Land of My Cradle Days

**A touching and evocative account of
growing up during the World War II
years and after in rural Ireland.
These were the final days of the old way of
life, before modernisation diminished the
self-reliance and community spirit which
had been the mainstay of rural living.
Here are the 'characters', the daily events,
the dependence on farm animals, the
routines and also the celebrations and
festivities, vividly recalled.**

MARTIN MORRISSEY
Raised on a farm in west Clare, between the towns of
Miltown-Malbay and Kilrush. Emigrated to New
York in the late 1950s and worked there as a travel
agent until his return to Ireland in the early 1970s,
where he worked in Cork with a multi-national company as sales and development manager. He is now a
freelance travel agent, living in Clare.

AN O'BRIEN PRESS BOOK

To Peggy and Marty

Land of My Cradle Days

MARTIN MORRISSEY

THE O'BRIEN PRESS
DUBLIN

FIRST PUBLISHED 1990 BY THE O'BRIEN PRESS
LTD., 20 VICTORIA ROAD, DUBLIN 6.
COPYRIGHT © MARTIN MORRISSEY

BRITISH LIBRARY CATALOGUING IN PUBLICATION DATA
MORRISSEY, MARTIN LAND OF MY CRADLE DAYS: RECOL-
LECTIONS FROM A COUNTRY CHILDHOOD 1. (REPUBLIC)
IRELAND. RURAL REGIONS. SOCIAL LIFE, 1942-1949 - BIO-
GRAPHIES I. TITLE 941.70822092

ISBN 0-86278-229-5

THE O'BRIEN PRESS RECEIVES ASSISTANCE FROM THE
ARTS COUNCIL/AN CHOMHAIRLE EALAÍON.

TYPESET AT THE O'BRIEN PRESS. COVER ILLUSTRATION:
MARIE HANLON. COVER DESIGN: MICHAEL O'BRIEN
COVER SEPARATIONS: THE CITY OFFICE, DUBLIN.
PRINTED BY THE GUERNSEY PRESS CO. LTD.

Contents

1 Making Do - There's a War On! 7

2 The Smell of New-mown Hay 15

3 Saving Hay Is Thirsty Work! 23

4 Being Good Isn't Easy 31

5 First Temptations 38

6 The Main Course Is Bacon! 46

7 Farm Friends 65

8 The End of the Summer Holidays 72

9 Preparing for Winter 83

10 Christmas Day Is Family Day 94

11 The Wren Dance 101

12 A Broken Wing 112

13 The Teacher and The Kaiser 118

14 Love and Marriage 124

15 The Harvest of the Strand 129

16 A Shepherd to a Mixed Flock 139

17 The Parish Mission 145

18 A Man and His Horse 148

CHAPTER 1

Making Do - There's a War On!

World War II was raging in Europe. Paris had fallen. Armies were on the move. Bombs rained from the skies over London, Bremen, Cologne and other cities. Convoys zig-zagged across the Atlantic, pursued by packs of U-boats. The dogs of war snarled around our coastline and sometimes droned across our skies. But Ireland remained neutral, never seeing the ugly face of war.

The side effects of being located on the edge of war-torn Europe were very real nevertheless. Scarcity of food and household goods was the main problem. It may sound a little easy, but for a nation of peaceful, ill-prepared people it was a very real hardship. The small farming communities of rural Ireland were still staggering from the effects of the economic war of the 1930s and were given no time to recover before war broke out in 1939.

In later life we came to realise that the early forties were years of fears, rumours, shortages, improvisations and adversities. But national adversity is a strange phenomenon. It brings out the best in the majority of people, knitting communities together. It makes people aware of the value of having a good neighbour, of being a good neighbour and of helping and sharing.

To those of us who were young children in the early forties the life of scarcity and shortage was accepted as normal, because we knew no other life. And in all fairness, country children had many advantages over town and city children, even though we believed the opposite was the case. Most of our food was home-produced – plenty of bacon, poultry, cabbage, turnips, carrots, parsnips, potatoes, much of our own flour, and of course there was plenty of milk. In summertime, nature provided us with our own sweet-counter – blackberries, gooseberries, currants and, in the early morning dew, some speckled fields of mushrooms. At meal-times, we soon learned to empty every plate put in front of us. We may have had dislikes for certain dishes or an aversion to some of the vegetables, but our choice was eat or go hungry. There were no other options, no substitutes.

The world knows the 1939-45 war as World War II, but in Ireland, possibly reflecting our neutrality, we diminished its importance by simply calling it 'The Emergency'. A new vocabulary evolved – we had emergency rationing, emergency petrol, emergency tillage, emergency turf, the word 'emergency' elevating everything to new national importance! Emergency laws were rushed through the Dáil, creating new emergency ministries, the Minister for Supplies being the most important.

Our area of west Clare had much in common with many places along the west coast of Ireland. The land was poor, the holdings were small and the work was hard. A mere thirty acres was considered a medium-sized farm. Farm sizes were quoted in the number of cows the land could maintain – 'the grass of seven cows' or 'a ten-cow farm'. Those small farmers, with their backs to the Atlantic, felt isolated and forgotten, perhaps with good reason. At one point in the forties, three of Clare's four TDs lived in Dublin! Though never seen until election time, they were fanatically supported by their respective party followers. In our own seaside parish, there were two tiny villages, a creamery, two small stations on the narrow-gauge West Clare railway, and one tarred road stretching from the town, five miles away, to about half a mile past our house. We had three priests, eight schools, a Garda barracks and no doctor – the local doctor lived four miles away at Spanish Point. It was an era when the priests were respected, the masters admired and the Guards feared.

In an effort to ensure the fair distribution of essential items, rationing was introduced. Every person was issued with a ration book, with coupons for the various items. The ration cards were deposited with the local shopkeeper which meant that one could shop only at that particular establishment. The size of each person's quota was meagre and encouraged the use of some shady schemes. In a few cases, some long-dead family members were 'resurrected' to gain an extra ration book, and in others recently deceased people did not have their books cancelled and were allowed to 'live on' for the duration of rationing. The extra few ounces of tea or the extra pound of sugar far outweighed any fear of future fire and brimstone.

The scarcity of cigarettes hit smokers very badly. They were at the mercy of the goodwill of the unfortunate shopkeeper who got only a fraction of normal supply and who usually tried their best to distribute them fairly among their customers. The 'small Woodbine' – an open-ended paper packet of five cigarettes costing two old pennies was the great favourite. The cigarette bush telegraph was highly efficient. The news of the arrival of a fresh supply to some shop spread like wildfire and smokers from miles around converged on the shop and begged, pleaded or cajoled the shopkeeper into letting them purchase a few 'fags'. I would venture a guess that more shoe leather was worn looking for cigarettes than for any other commodity. Each cigarette was good for two or three smokes – just a few drags, then it was 'topped' until it was time for the next smoke. The butts were hoarded in top pockets and when supplies ran short a makeshift cigarette could be made from two or three butts rolled in a piece of paper. When real desperation set in, 'cigarettes' were made from brown paper, tea leaves or even from turf dust. Many the lip was burned or moustache singed from such experiments! And the day of the black market had arrived. A few traders seized the opportunity to make a fast profit charging at least one old penny per cigarette (and an exorbitant pound note for a pound of tea). The black market introduced some unfamiliar brand names – Players Weights, Capstan, Craven A, White Horse and a few Turkish brands. The latter earned themselves some uncomplimentary nicknames and gave rise to comments such as, 'Sure, you'd need the jaws of an ass to knock a pull out of that fag.'

For the housewife, baking bread was the biggest problem. White flour had disappeared and was replaced by a brown bran flour of poor quality, making baking a nightmare. Small quantities of farm-grown wheat were crushed and ground at a stone mill near the town. The mill was water-powered, with a mill race, a water wheel and huge grinding stones. Fine-meshed riddles, strainers and even silk stockings were used in an effort to remove some of the bran and husks from the flour. Even the meagre ration of flour from the shops was of poor quality. The resulting bread was a black-brown unpalatable hard cake. For some people the 'black bread' proved a disaster. Although it became the source of many jokes and funny stories, its extremely laxative effects were not a laughing matter for the unfortunate victims. A neighbour summed it up when he said that he dreaded working in the centre of a field because that was the furthest point from the headland! Many of those most allergic to the purgative powers of the black bread survived on a diet of potatoes for several years. But every cloud has a silver lining. The empty flour bags were a boon to the housewife. After washing and bleaching, she had some precious cloth which was converted into tea-towels, bed sheets and even undergarments for children. Nothing was wasted, not even the thread that had been used in making the bags.

The land in our area is not suited to the production of corn. It is good for summer and autumn grazing, but because of an impervious layer of mud close to the surface, drainage is poor, giving way to rushy fields and clusters of what are known locally as 'fellastrums'. That layer of yellow clinging mud is better known by its old Irish name, the *dó buí*. The imposition of compulsory tillage in the early forties put extra hardship on the small farmers who needed every foot of their arable land for grazing and meadowing. Crop returns were predictably poor. The few acres they were forced to plough were used mainly for barley and oats and only very little wheat. Many farmers had their potato gardens in black-earth plots or 'strips' which were rented annually and often some distance from home. Now, parts of those strips were turned over to the growing of sugar beet, a cash crop. At the local railway station, the open wagons were loaded with the beet, ensuring a small cheque within a few weeks. The beet harvest provided a welcome boost for the grower – the foliage was used immediately as fodder for the cattle, the returned beet pulp was used over the winter months and the cheque was very welcome.

The advent of compulsory tillage, however undesirable, had a positive effect on the skills of ploughing and gave rise to a competitive spirit which resulted in the annual local ploughing match. Those competitions opened up a new avenue of conversation – the merits and demerits of the drill plough, the swing plough, the wheel plough, the angle of the knife to the coulter, or the methods of ploughing new ground (the bawn) as compared with the methods of ploughing stubble. And of course the importance of the horse reached a new height. In fact, the horse was coming into its own. A few owned a Clydesdale, but this type was considered too big for the small farmer. Thus came the era of the most beloved of all Irish horses, the Irish draught horse. We had such a horse, Grey Fann, a big gentle animal who never seemed to tire and was almost like one of the family. She was treated like a pet and seemed to love human company. She would follow my father around the fields and if she felt she was not getting enough attention, would gently lift the hat from his head and walk after him holding the hat by its brim in her mouth.

With rationing in operation, new clothes were almost impossible to get, even for those who had money. The parcels from America were no longer arriving. Working clothes, trousers in particular, were of soft poor quality and the sewing on of patches became an art in itself. But a new development helped to alleviate the problem for a few. Two new voluntary groups were formed to defend our coasts against invasion: the Local Defence Force, the LDF, and its poorer relation, the Local Security Force, the LSF. To many they were a God-sent blessing. The equipment handed out was worth a few inconveniences! A new uniform was issued each year with interim replacements for items damaged in 'the line of duty'. The heavy green woollen trousers appeared to have the greatest number of casualties. The tunics, berets and the oilskin capes were not suited to everyday farm wear and therefore had a much longer life. The trousers and the heavy brown boots were the real prizes. Marching and drilling was a small price to pay and in fact proved a mild relief from the humdrum of farming. The recruits trained for a year or more with timber 'guns' before being issued with some rifles. The road past our school was a favourite marching area. The coast was only half a mile away, with plenty of sand dunes suitable for mock battles and 'manoeuvres'. During our lunch break and on our way home from school, we too marched and played soldiers, shouting 'Left, right, left, right', 'about turn' or 'attention', just as we saw the adults do.

One morning a platoon of the local LDF marched past the school, very erect, swinging their arms and going towards the coast. Everybody in the school was talking about the news that a big German mine was floating in the sea very close to the shore. Even though it was more than half a mile away, there was some hopeful speculation that should it explode, it might be strong enough to knock the school or at least cause it sufficient damage to force it to close and give us all a good holiday. At the eleven o'clock break, the men were back again, sitting on the grassy bank opposite the school. A lot of banter was going on about their marksmanship. We lined the school wall, admiring their smart uniforms and listening to them. It appeared that on reaching the beach, they took up position on top of the sand dunes and, on command, fired a fusilade of bullets at the mine! Fortunately for all concerned, they peppered the water all round the target but the mine floated on unscathed. They had only two bullets each anyway. One of them remarked loudly, 'Lads, 'twas a good thing we ran out of ammunition or we wouldn't have a mackerel left in the sea.' While they guffawed, there was an almighty boom, rattling the school windows and shaking the ground under our feet. A brilliant flash lit the beach area. The mine had struck the rocks and exploded. We were very frightened.

Our local heroes didn't look too happy either. The fun and banter stopped. They just had seen a fleeting glimpse of the ugly face of war! The next horned mine that drifted towards the shore some time later was made the responsibility of the regular army. No pair of trousers was worth that kind of risk! Meanwhile they trained and marched and drilled, watching and waiting for an invasion that never came.

CHAPTER 2

The Smell of New-mown Hay

The hay-making season was probably the busiest time of the year for my father, but to me, as a child, it was a wonderful time. It was the height of summer with long warm sunny days, blue skies and larks singing in the air. Gentle breezes rippled the tall hay in the meadows, creating undulating waves as though the hay were being caressed by a giant invisible hand. It was the season when I was at last allowed to kick off my boots and stockings and run barefoot through the fields, play in the hay and get plenty of horseback rides on Grey Fann. After a week of walking around barefoot, the feet were no longer soft and tender. It was exhilarating to run in the fresh grass, to feel the warm mud squelching through my toes or to paddle in the stream at the bottom of our land beside the Long Meadow, trying to catch tadpoles in a jam jar.

Preparations for saving the hay began in leisurely fashion. In early June, the machinery was pulled out into the yard from the back of the long car-house beside the house. First out was the Deering mowing machine, with the cogged iron wheels and the blade-comb with its long pointed teeth or fingers. It had a metal seat, a few hand levers that I did not understand and a foot pedal for raising or lowering the cutting blade when in use. The gear wheels made a strange clicking noise when turned or reversed. Father oiled and checked every part. He had an oilcan with a long spout which squirted oil into axles, gears and connecting-rod. Next the long drawing chains were taken down from their nail on the car-house wall and cleaned. A strip of cloth was bandaged around the centre of each chain to make sure they would not chafe Grey Fann's sides. The horse's tackling was checked carefully and any frayed strap replaced. Extra-special attention was given to the horse collar, not so much to the hames to which the chains would be attached but to the padding of the collar itself. Any rips or frayed ends would cause chafing or 'galding' to the neck and shoulders of a sweating horse. Father often said, 'Look after your horse and he will never let you down. Only people let you down.'

If he found that the padding cover of the collar was not to his satisfaction, father took immediate steps to replace it. This signalled a time for me to keep a low profile. Going into the kitchen he opened the doors of the press under the glass case where he kept many of his small tools and nails. For this particular job he was looking for an awl, a saddler's needle, some hemp thread and a ball of black wax. If he didn't find them at the first attempt, instant frustration set in. Old biscuit tins and shoe boxes full of nails, washers, bits of bicycle chains, pieces of copper wire and old rusty screws, were tumbled onto the flagged floor. Finding nothing, the contents were quickly shoved back in the container in glorious disarray and put back in the press. Several tall narrow round tins advertising Van Hooten's cocoa got the same treatment until at last the muttering and swearing subsided. He had found the missing items. Closing the press, he got off his knees, telling nobody in particular that he 'wished to God that people would stop moving his things around'. During all this commotion, my mother would sit by the fire, watching serenely and waiting for the storm to run its course. After he had gone out to the car-house, she would quietly clean up the dust and debris strewn about the floor near the press. If I appeared a little apprehensive, she dismissed the whole incident by telling me that 'Dad tends to become a little excitable at times, but there's no harm in him.' When I mentioned that I had heard Dad swearing a lot, she said, 'Dad wasn't really cursing – that's his way of asking God to find what he was looking for.' To a six-year-old, her explanation was acceptable. I found this information useful on some occasions after that when I noticed that Dad became exceptionally holy for a few minutes if something was going wrong, such as a stupid cow running off down the road instead of turning in through the open gate!

Meanwhile out in the car-house, Dad had stripped off the old collar lining and smoothed the straw padding. Up in the garret where he kept all the bigger spare bits and pieces – his 'thrumpery' as my mother called it – he had a roll of white flannel collar lining with little blue squares. He cut out the two strips he needed, one for each side of the collar and then waxed some lengths of the hemp thread with the little ball of wax. Using the awl to bore a series of tiny holes in the thick leather, he deftly worked with the saddler's needle to stitch on the new lining. Within an hour, the collar was like new. Dad was a man of many talents, a fact I did not appreciate until many years later. At that young age, I assumed that all fathers were the same.

He kept a careful watch on the growth of the meadows. We had five meadows, each with its own name – the small Shan Gort, the Red Gate, Connell's Meadow, the Cross Meadow at the back of the house and the Long Meadow in the valley by the stream.

The evening before the first meadow, the Shan Gort, was

cut, the two long blades were taken down from the garret. Balancing the blade across his knees, Dad sharpened each triangular section with a file until it was razor sharp. About fifteen such sections were rivetted to a long thin metal bar to make up the saw-toothed mowing blade. Usually after about an hour's cutting, the sharpness of the blade became dulled and was replaced by the spare blade.

When the morning chores were finished and the dew had been evaporated by the warm sun, Dad decreed that it was 'time to make a start, *in ainm Dé.*' Grey Fann was tackled to the machine. Mother produced the big bottle of holy water and, with the aid of the usual long feather from the wing of a goose, the horse, the machine and Dad and I were sprinkled liberally. I got a stern lecture about staying well clear of the cutting blade. I sat on Dad's lap in the springing seat of the mowing machine and he let me drive Grey Fann back the Clune road, which formed the northern boundary of our farm, until we reached the gate of the Shan Gort. Taking the scythe from where he had it tied on the machine, he sharpened it with a few deft strokes of the scythe-board. He caught the scythe by its two protruding handles, or 'durneens', and bending his back he swung it back and forth, cutting a small area inside the gate to make room for the horse and mower. This avoided trampling on, or 'possing', the standing hay. Every scrap of hay could be valuable in the coming winter!

The blade-comb was lowered into the horizontal cutting position, the long blade was pushed into place, the connecting rod was locked into the eye of the blade, the machine was put in gear and all was ready. Dad sat up on the metal seat, with a small cushion of hay under him. Picking up the long reins, he blessed himself and gave the word to Grey Fann to start. They moved off, the blade now a silver blur before it disappeared into the retreating wall of standing hay. They moved clockwise around the meadow, keeping close to the briar-covered wall. I stood by the gate watching them until they had four or five rounds completed. I had been given a very important job to do. With a light hay rake, I cleared away the first ray of the new-mown hay. Later on, moving anti-clockwise, the machine would cut down the back 'raheen' close by the walls. Small patches such as corners, called 'fushocks', would have to be cut with the scythe as the machine couldn't reach them.

The staccato crackle of the machine filled the meadow with its musical sound. The unforgettable smell of new-mown hay filled our nostrils. The square of still-standing hay grew steadily smaller as Grey Fann plodded her way round and round. Suddenly the machine stopped. I watched closely, full of curiosity as Dad jumped off the seat and retraced his steps a little, frantically waving a fistful of long hay in front of his face. He knelt down quickly on one knee. He had uncovered a wild beehive. Still waving the hay, he picked up the honeycomb and ran to where I stood by the gate. The angry bees had given up the chase by then. As we shared the prize, he told me a few stories about bees and how they collected the nectar for the honey. It was one of those small rare moments that one never forgets. I felt a little sorry for the hardworking bees, but if we had not taken the honey the watchful crows would have robbed the hive within a few minutes.

When we got home, Dad gave Grey Fann a quick rub down to dry off the sweat marks of the tackling, then he turned her loose into her field. She rolled herself several times in the lush green grass and galloped around the field as though she was telling all and sundry that she was not the least bit tired after her day's work.

Within a day or two, the hot summer sun had bleached and

dried the top layer of the new-mown hay. It was time to turn over the neat rows. The heavy Bamford hay-tosser was prepared. The big spindly iron wheels towered over me. The revolving drums built around the axle had rows of long iron spikes or 'fingers'. A wide shield of corrugated galvanised iron protected the driver from the swirling spikes. Standing on the narrow platform at the front of the tosser, Dad guided Grey Fann around the meadow, taking in two rows at a time. Plucked from the ground and tossed several feet in the air, the hay fell back down in a fluffy cascade. In those years, the tosser was a reasonably new labour-saving invention that freed many hours which would otherwise have been spent turning the hay with the two-pronged fork.

When the hay had dried for a few hours in the sunshine, Grey Fann was hitched to the raking machine with its long row of large circular claw-like teeth. When the teeth had collected a full roll of hay, the hand lever was pulled back, leaving the roll on the ground before going to collect the next roll. In this way the hay was gathered into long thick rows, or 'rays', the full length of the meadow, exposing the freshly cut white-green stubble for the first time. By going along the length of the rays, it was very easy to collect the hay into a series of mounds around the meadow. When that was completed, Grey Fann was untackled and let loose to graze as she wished. With the hay from the fluffy mounds, my father began building hay-cocks, or 'trams', with the two-pronged fork. It was hot dusty work, with hay seed matting one's hair and getting down the back of one's shirt, making it a very itchy business. I loved the making of the trams because I could help. I jumped into the middle of the tram when it was quite low and trampled down the hay. Dad lifted up great forkfuls that knocked me over, causing many a good laugh. As the tram grew higher, it got narrower. It became more and more difficult to retain my balance as the tram wobbled and jiggled under me. By now I was on my knees, balancing myself like a tightrope walker. On the rare occasion that a tram fell, Dad always caught me before I hit the ground. When he deemed the tram was completed, he combed it down gently with the hand rake, knocking off any loose hay. He then threw me a *súgán*, or band, which he tied around a 'twist' of hay on opposite sides of the tram. Two bands were put on each tram, making them safe against any wind that might rise. Putting a leg on either side of one of the bands, I slid down the side of the tram into his waiting arms. We worked happily until all the hay was trammed and securely tied down. The following morning, the next meadow was cut and the process continued until we finally reached the last one, the Long Meadow.

When a meadow was being trammed, we stayed in the field for our lunch. My father never used a watch while he was working, but he could tell the time by the height of the sun. Even on cloudy days he could read nature's clock. I tried hard to master this art, without too much success. My tummy was my best clock – if I was really hungry, it must be close to either one o'clock or six o'clock! But Dad would look up at the sun and say to me, 'Your mother will be here soon with the tea.' And every time, without fail, she would appear at the gate within a few minutes.

There is something special about having a meal in a hayfield. Everything seems to be twice as tasty. Even the hayseed and the occasional inquisitive fly did not detract from the enjoyment. The long slices of griddle bread with plenty of butter and the pieces of apple cake were all so much better than at home. Mother always brought the tea in a white enamel can with a tight lid, and the big message-bag held the bread, cups, spoons and a bottle of milk. She spread a tea-towel in the shade of a tram and laid out the lunch on it. There was never any need to call us twice. I was not too fond of tea, but in the meadow I always had a cup of the strong brew so loved by both of them. Even that tasted good!

CHAPTER 3

Saving Hay
Is Thirsty Work!

The magic formula for producing good quality hay is that it should be cut, dried and stacked into trams without rain having fallen on it. This was every farmer's ambition as he worked in the meadows with 'one eye on the hay and one eye on the sky'. Four of our five meadows were of average size, between two and three acres. My father saved the hay in those meadows on his own, even though I felt at the time that I was making an invaluable contribution. With hindsight, I'm sure I was more a hindrance than a help.

Saving the hay in the Long Meadow always called for a mighty effort. Cutting the eight acres was a full day's work and by the time she arrived back in the yard in the evening Grey Fann was exhausted despite the many rest periods Dad let her have. Usually she decided for herself when to take a breather. They worked together with extraordinary understanding. All his orders were verbal, using the reins only to guide her but never to jerk or check her. On reaching the end of one cut, he would shout 'Whee', and she would stop. To turn the right-angled corner in order to line up the machine for the next cut, he would tell her 'Turn in'. Now and then she ignored this order and stood still for a minute getting her breath back, her tail swishing at the flies. When she was ready, she turned in of her own accord and continued moving until she needed another break. He often stopped the machine and went to the stream to get a drink from the tin-can or from the bottle of milk where the babbling waters of the stream kept it cool. He always carried back a bucket of water for Grey Fann so that she too could refresh herself.

When the Long Meadow was cut down, the saving of the hay was a source of anxiety. And, without fail, a couple of the neighbours always arrived to help with the gathering in and the making of the trams. The extra help made all the difference. This time-honoured system of helping each other, or 'coring', was vital to the survival of the small farmer. Today they helped Dad; some other day he would help them with one of their meadows. A feature of coring was that the help was never asked for or demanded, but watchful neighbours knew when help was most needed. When Dad had turned and made rows of the hay, our two nearest neighbours arrived, bringing their own two-pronged pitch forks. I was quietly sent to tell Mother of the two extra mouths to be catered for at dinner-time and again at the four o'clock evening tea. With the neighbours' help, the Long Meadow was no longer intimidating. I often heard my father say, 'You can have your relations, but give me a good neighbour any time.'

When neighbours came to help in the meadow, there was usually one addition to the beverages. Apart from the normal drinks of tea and milk to quench the thirst during the heat of the day, a special treat of a gallon of stout, or porter as it was called, was produced for the friends, usually after the four o'clock tea. It was considered too gassy for consumption earlier in the day! Even though fizzy lemonade was my favourite drink, I knew what stout tasted like because on a few occasions friends or visitors had offered me a little sip from their glasses. I didn't like it very much as it was very sharp and bitter. And I had seen some men, after a few glasses of stout, get drunk and begin to sing loudly.

On one beautiful July day the two neighbours were helping Dad in the Long Meadow and I was sent to the village to get the stout for the men. It made me feel good to be given such responsibility. I was quite capable of going to the village on my own because I was getting to be a big boy now, six-and-a-half years, going on seven! I ran most of the way, swinging the empty sweet-gallon, with the money, wrapped in paper, clutched tightly in my hand. I felt quite important as I explained my mission to the woman in the public house. She was a relative of my mother's and she gave me a small glass of lemonade.

The return journey was much slower. It was mostly uphill and the can was fairly heavy. It was such a hot day. I ambled along, churning up little dust clouds with my bare feet and watching out for unfriendly dogs. I risked spilling some of the stout when I ran as fast as possible past the narrow road which led up to the graveyard on the hill. Even though 'they' would not be out and about in broad daylight, there was no point in tempting fate. I had heard too many ghost stories about 'them'.

Reaching the top of the last hill, within sight of home, I had to take a rest and get my breath back. My fingers were almost numb from the handle of the can. I felt very hot and very thirsty. I would have loved a second glass of that lemonade or even a small drink of water. My throat was parched and my mouth felt like cotton wool. I suddenly thought that it was more than likely that at least one of the men was sure to offer me a sip of stout from his glass as soon as I reached the meadow. After considering the thought for a moment, I decided to accept the invitation before it was even made. Just one small mouthful to wet my dry tongue! I moved to the high grass at the side of the road and sat down against the cool grassy ditch. Removing the tight lid, I raised the can to my lips and took a good gulp. I gagged on the bitter taste, coughing and spluttering, and spilled most of that mouthful down the front of my shirt. I had to wait for a minute to get my composure back. By that time, it seemed to me that this stuff was not really as horrible as I had always thought. As I had spilled most of it, I decided that the first mouthful didn't count. And it was so cool. I gingerly tried a second mouthful, this time a much smaller one. Yes, the taste had improved! I would have one more mouthful, well, maybe a second one and then I would go to the meadow. I was amazing myself — I could drink stout just like the big men. I tried drinking three or four mouthfuls, one after the other, as I had seen the men do. I was able to do it! This was great! My thirst was gone, well, almost gone. I had one or two more long drinks until I could take no more. I was so full! My tummy felt like it was going to burst. I had quite a job getting the lid back on the can. It didn't seem to fit too well anymore! I noticed that the level of the stout seemed to have gone down a lot since I had opened the can. How was I going to explain that? I would have to think about that some more!

I knew I should have been very worried but somehow or other it didn't seem to matter. I felt tired and lethargic. I lay back in the grass for a minute, and had a strange feeling that I was no longer lying on the grass but floating on a cloud up in the blue sky, going up and down, up and down, up and down! I wanted to get off this see-saw right now because the cloud was also starting to go round and round! I sat up quickly. My head felt terrible! A sudden pain shot between my eyes as though somebody was driving a nail through me. The top of my head was throbbing. My ears were popping and my eyes were watering, blurring my vision. My tongue felt funny, as though it was twice its normal size or else it was turned upside down. I was sweating but I felt cold. What was wrong, what was happening to me? Suddenly my tummy started to heave. Before I realised what was happening, I became violently ill in the high grass. I felt awful! My mind had become very muddled as I struggled to understand what was going on. I could not be drunk because on the few occasions I had seen men getting drunk, they always seemed to be very jolly and wanting to sing. I didn't feel jolly, nor did I feel like singing. In fact I felt utterly miserable! A terrible thought stuck me! If I wasn't drunk, then I must be dying. Suddenly I remembered what my teacher, the Missus, had told us about some people dying and going down to Hell with all those big fires. I wasn't sure if they sent small boys down there. The idea of being the first didn't appeal to me. It was actually the thought of all those small little devils in Hell, shovelling loads of red-hot coals on top of my head that galvanised me into taking drastic action. If only I could get as far as Dad and Mother as fast as possible, I was sure they would save me from such a terrible event!

I jumped to my feet, only to discover that the whole world was swaying from side to side and everything looked blurred. I dropped to one knee, waiting for the world to steady itself. The swaying stopped. Standing up, I began to walk very carefully towards home with the can of stout in one hand. Apart from the occasional sway, the ground was steady again. My confidence grew even though my head was still throbbing. The fear of dying and going down to Hell was receding with every step. Leaving the road, I walked across the fields, along the banks of the stream that flowed by the Long Meadow. But the fading thoughts of dying were suddenly replaced by the thoughts of what my father would say when he noticed the missing stout. I stopped and lifted the lid. The smell was nauseating! I felt like being sick again. How could I have swallowed that awful stuff? How could grown-ups drink it and pretend to like it so much?

The can was only a little over half full. He definitely would notice! I knelt on the bank of the stream beside the can, weighing up the pros and cons. If I told Dad the truth, I would get walloped, right there in front of the two neighbours. If I said nothing, he would know anyway and I would get a walloping later on that night at home. Neither option was very attractive but the second seemed to be the better of the two because the neighbours would not be present to add to my humiliation. I suddenly saw the answer to my problems – the stream! Using the lid as a ladle, I filled up the can with water. I could see it was not the ideal solution but beggars can't be choosers! I could see the bottom of the can fairly clearly through the diluted mixture. And the stout was more brown than black! I stirred it frantically with a piece of a stick until the froth covered the top. I knew what I was doing was not right but the emergency situation I was in left no room for moral arguments!

I waited until my father was at the far end of the Long Meadow before I ventured over the fence. Discretion suggested that I should keep well out of his way for the moment as he would surely hear the hammering that still went on inside my head and he might start asking some very awkward questions! I shouted at our neighbour, Michael, to get his attention. My voice was hoarse and unrecognisable, and my throat hurt. A fast retreat was essential! Michael waved to me and I left the can on the ground where they could see it. I ran home as fast as my poor head would allow. Mother saw me coming into the yard and asked what had delayed me. Before I could even think up a suitable reply, she pressed me further.

Normally my mother was very gentle and placid but when she wanted to she was capable of being quite strict. Eyeing me suspiciously, she questioned me about the condition of my clothes, especially my shirt which smelled like a brewery. She remarked that I didn't look very well and was I feeling all right? I couldn't lie to her. I blurted out the whole story, especially about my almost dying on the side of the road. She assured me that I was not going to die and that God had decided to give me another chance to be good. I resolved to accept God's kind offer. She made me drink two cups of hot milk to cure me, even though I detested the taste of it. It was almost as sickening as the stout, but within a very short time I was feeling much better. Even my head had stopped throbbing and I was beginning to feel like my old self.

But I was not out of the woods yet. She gave me an almighty lecture about the bold thing I had done and how unfair I had been to the men who were working hard in the meadow. I felt very ashamed of my behaviour. She told me later on, in her own gentle way, about the evils of drink and how some men made fools of themselves by drinking too much. 'Your Dad very rarely takes a drink and it would make me very happy if you kept well away from it when you grow up,' she said. I assured her that I now hated stout and that I was going 'on the dry' from that very day. The mention of Dad reminded me that he would be home in a couple of hours. I knew that I would be severely punished and I now accepted the fact that I deserved it. But I must try to postpone it for at least a day or two! By that time he mightn't be as angry. I pleaded with Mother not to tell him my sad story when he returned. She appeared unmoved. I continued pleading. At last, a tiny glimmer of hope! She said, 'We'll see!'

Later that evening, he arrived back in the yard. I went out of my way to be very helpful, bringing in the turf, helping

Mother lay the table and volunteering to assist in all the chores. I felt his eyes on me several times but he never said a word. There wasn't a mention about the stout, about the water being added to it or even about my leaving the Long Meadow so quickly. I found this much worse than getting punished immediately. At least that would be over and finished. Now I didn't know from minute to minute when the axe was going to fall. On the following day, I kept up a constant chatter whenever I was in his company – and still not a word about the can of stout. After a few days of this awful strain, I felt that the danger was receding and that he had now forgotten about it. As a matter of fact, it was many years later when we remembered that particular incident. I discovered that he knew the whole story and had rather enjoyed it. He had decided that keeping me in suspense was the best method of teaching me a good lesson. He was absolutely right – a walloping would have been forgotten very quickly!

CHAPTER 4

'Being Good Isn't Easy!'

I could have been sent to any of three schools, each of them about a mile and a half from home. One was chosen over the others for no particular reason except that its Master lived just down the road from our house. It was an old two-teacher school, surrounded by a stone wall that cut many a climbing knee. The drab, grey building was surrounded by a small gravel yard with one very puddly corner. The sole entrance to the classrooms was through a porch attached to the western gable. One section of the porch was cordoned off by a low partition and used as a turf-house. The remaining tiny corridor inside the door had been given the grand title of 'cloakroom'. A few coats could be hung from the several long nails which had been hammered into the partition and the back of the door. The school was situated beside the West Clare railway tracks and the occasional passing train caused a flurry of excitement as it huffed and puffed up the slight incline before disappearing into the cutting near the top of the hill. Some of the more adventurous 'big lads' sneaked through the wires, if the Master was out of sight, and laid ha'pennies on the iron rails, hoping that they would be squashed big enough to be passed off as pennies in some shop where the interior lighting would be rather poor! It rarely worked. On the front wall of the school, in between the two high narrow windows, a grey limestone notice proclaimed to the passing world that this was 'Clonadrum N.S. Erected in 1854'. However, these being the war years, the words had been smeared with pink plaster, to deny the expected invading German army the knowledge that they had finally reached Clonadrum!

Even though we did not appreciate it at the time, we were blessed with two wonderful dedicated teachers who worked tirelessly, in primitive conditions, for the betterment of their pupils. We walked in awe through the Master's room to get to our own classroom where infants, first and second classes were packed together. The Missus was a good friend of my mother's, but I soon discovered that this friendship did not give me any privileges. She was a strict disciplinarian who accepted no nonsense from any of us, but was always kind and fair.

Preparing us for our First Communion was her doubtful privilege. Day after day we recited, in high-pitched sing-song voices, endless short prayers until we were word-perfect. She repeatedly told us that the little wafer in Holy Communion was Our Lord Himself, coming down from heaven, just to be with us. That fact was very hard to grasp, but if the Missus said so, then it was true! We learned that there were hundreds of sins, most of which we had never heard of before and did not understand. We learned the Confiteor and the long Act of Contrition. We practised receiving Communion with pieces of paper, sticking out our tongues, reverently for a change. Making one's Confession was rehearsed constantly, with the Missus sitting on a chair listening to our mock Confessions as we knelt beside her. Most of us thought it was great fun, but there were no outbursts of laughter under the eagle eye of the Missus. We learned that every sin, even the smallest, put a little black spot on our soul and that the priest in the Confessional, with one wave of his hand while saying some words in Latin, wiped them all away, leaving our souls shining brightly once more. Examining our consciences was the most difficult task as one needed a great memory. But the Missus gave us a long list of possible transgressions that might jog our memories – not saying our morning or night prayers, telling lies, name-calling, looking around us in church, disobeying our parents or teachers, and so on. The list seemed endless. As we had to tell the priest something, we chose a few at random, deciding among ourselves that three or four seemed just about the right number, not too long and not too short!

As the great occasion drew nearer, excitement began to mount. Mother had got me a new suit, new stockings with turned-down tops and a new pair of Little Duke boots that creaked with every step. Our Confessions were to be held on a Friday, with First Communion on the following day. The days before our First Confession were filled with the revision of all the prayers we had been learning, and we were constantly examined and questioned by the Missus. Even the Master came in to test us. Being afraid of the Master made us stumble and stutter, as we knew that he had the power to keep us back for another year if we didn't know our prayers properly. On the Thursday, the parish priest, Father O', came to talk to us and asked us a few questions. He looked very happy with us. But the Missus was not going to sit back on her laurels. She kept us reciting the prayers until it was time to go home. There were so many different prayers to remember. There were prayers before Confession and prayers after, prayers before Communion and prayers after, prayers to say for our teachers, our parents, the Pope and for peace. Some of the bigger children in the Master's room made fun at our expense, calling us 'angels' and 'holy Joes' and asking us what we were going to tell the priest in Confession. But the Missus had told us that our Confessions were private and should not be told to others.

Walking home from school one evening I talked about the upcoming Confession day with my cousin, Gerry. He was in sixth class and of course we knew that all the big lads were very clever and knew everything. He asked me what I was going to tell the priest. I wanted my Confession to sound good and to make an impression on the priest, and I felt that Gerry was the ideal person to give me his opinion. I told him the four sins I had chosen and had been practising. He was shaking his head. 'I don't know about those,' he said. 'I think they're very ordinary. They'll all have the same old things to tell the priest.' We walked on a little further. I was feeling a bit deflated. Suddenly he stopped and turned to me saying, 'You know something? I'll give you a sin I can guarantee not one of the others will have.' I was more than interested. I needed this one badly! 'Didn't you often wish that the Missus was sick some morning and couldn't be in school for a couple of days?' he asked. I agreed that the thought had crossed my mind on a few occasions. 'Well,' says Gerry, 'That's a small sin and the name for it is "carnal knowledge". Will you be able to remember that?' I had never heard those big words before but I could see that Gerry knew what he was talking about. It sounded very important and we practised the words until we got to his gateway. He warned me not to tell the others, especially the Missus. I readily agreed as there was no point in sharing my moment of glory. I repeated the new sin all the way home, until I was sure I would remember it.

The fateful Friday arrived. We didn't have to go to school, which made the day a success even before it began. The Missus had given us dire warning to be at the church at eleven o'clock. I wore my ordinary school clothes as the new outfit was reserved for the following day, First Communion day. I walked to the village, mentally revising all my prayers and my well-rehearsed list of sins. The Missus was already there, talking to Father O'. She divided us into two groups, the girls sitting near one side of the Confession box, the boys at the other side. I found myself sitting at the end of the boys' seat, nearest to the box. I would have preferred not to be the first as it would have been comforting to know how a few of the others fared before having to take the plunge. Despite this disadvantage, I decided to make the most of it and set such a high standard it would be difficult for the others to follow in my footsteps. Father O' entered the centre door of the box and sat down, closing the door behind him. My heart began to pound with apprehension.

The first girl went into the right-hand side of the box and then the Missus beckoned to me to go into the left-hand side. The girl and Father O' were already in deep whispered conversation. Opening the door, I entered the penitential box for the first time. There was a small kneeler on the floor, a short shelf on which to rest one's arms and a wire mesh-covered opening through which I would tell my sins to the priest. I closed the door tightly so that the others on the outside would not hear my sins. It was pitch black inside. It was frightening for a few moments. I felt around with my hands until I found the kneeler, and knelt down carefully. Straightening myself up, I banged my head on the underside of the shelf. The shelf was level with the tip of my nose. How could I talk to the priest with my mouth below the level of the shelf? This was not going to work. I wriggled about, trying to stretch myself upwards to get closer to the wire mesh. But the kneeler tipped over and I fell in a most ungainly heap on the flat of my back on the floor with my two legs up in the air! The door flew open. The Missus stood there glaring at me, the sunlight glinting on her glasses. 'Conduct yourself in there,' she grated at me in a harsh whisper, 'or I'll deal with you later on.' Things were not going well at all! It might have been my First Confession but it seemed to be well on its way to being my last! The shock of falling off the kneeler was bad but I felt even worse when I heard the giggles of my fellow penitents on the outside!

I knew now that the kneeler was out of the question. I had to think up some other alternative! I put my arms on the shelf and, placing my feet as far back as I could, I stood with partially bent knees, at a most uncomfortable angle, with my face pressed against the wire grille. The waiting was unbearable! Would he ever stop talking and hurry up? I could feel my knees trembling with the strain. Suddenly I had an acute attack of 'pins and needles' in my right foot. I was in agony, hopping on one foot, when the shutter slid back with a bang and I could dimly see a part of Father O's shiny bald head as he said to me, 'God Bless you, my child. This is your First Confession.' I had lost my concentration and was totally confused. I answered him, 'Bless me, Father, for I have... I have... I have pins and needles in my leg, Father.' He seemed taken aback for a moment but, recovering quickly, he said, 'Take your time. They will go away in a minute.' He was right. In less than a minute, the pains had disappeared. I was warming to Father O'. He did not threaten me or put on a sour face like the Missus had done!

'Whenever you're ready, we'll start again,' Father O' told me gently. I got through the Confiteor without stumbling even once. My confidence had returned, and my concentration was fully restored. 'Now, tell me your sins,' said Father O'. I began my well-rehearsed list, trotting out first my three very average sins. I was keeping the best until last. With pride in my voice, I produced what I knew would be a certain winner – 'and I had carnal knowledge three times, Father.' 'You what?' he said in what seemed like a choked voice. I felt elated. I had impressed him even more than I had expected. 'What did you say again?' he asked in a much calmer voice. 'I had carnal knowledge three times,' I repeated. 'Tell me what you mean by that,' he asked. I was amazed that a man like him, a priest no less, didn't know the meaning of those big words and I was flattered that he was asking me, a small boy, to explain them to him. I explained the sin to him exactly as Gerry had told me the previous day on our way home from school. He listened very carefully before saying to me, 'Well now, you have been a very good boy and maybe you could do me a big favour. From now on when you come to Confession explain your sins to the priest in small words rather than using all those big long words. It would make the priest very happy. And tell me something while we're talking, who taught you those big words?' I didn't mind sharing the glory and honour with my cousin Gerry, so I told Father O' all about him. 'He must be a very clever boy,' he said. 'I think I had better have a little chat with him sometime.' I thought that was a very good idea too as it might do Father O' the world of good! He told me to say three Hail Marys for my penance and to pray for him. I told him I would.

I came out of the box into the blinding sunlight, with a great sense of well-being. The Missus was kneeling at the back seat. I looked apprehensively at her as I went to my appointed seat, two seats in front of hers. She glanced stern-faced at me and looked away. She must still be angry with me! Or maybe she had already forgotten! Just to be doubly sure, I put an extra large portion of devotion into the saying of my penance and the other prayers as I knelt with clasped hands and bowed head. I was hoping that she would notice my extreme piety.

CHAPTER 5

First Temptations!

With my First Confession more or less successfully completed, I left the church with a great sense of achievement and happiness. All those sins had been erased from my soul, and I felt myself full of goodness. This must be the sanctifying grace that the Missus was always talking about. I felt my chest expanding with pride as I sensed that everyone in the village was aware of my shining soul, without even the slightest stain on it.

While First Communion day may be a most important day, I was determined to celebrate my First Confession. I had money that was burning a hole in my pocket – a bright brown penny with a hen and her chickens on one side and a harp on the other. There was a small dark sweetshop, Annie Fitz's, in the village and I had heard that she had one brand of hard sweets that were ten for a penny. Annie was a small lovely lady with a smiling cherubic face and spectacles. She was a very religious person, and it was a well-known fact that if she believed that one was a well-behaved boy and a little inclined towards religion, an extra sweet was always thrown in for good measure. She was a very neat person and always handed the sweets over the counter in a funnel-shaped paper twist, a *tóisín*, the making of which she had brought to a fine art. She was fanatical in her efforts to collect money for the foreign missions, or 'collecting for the black babies' as she termed it. Any small change from the purchase of sweets was solicited for the 'poor black babies out in Africa who are often without a Mammy or a Daddy with only torn clothes and starving'. She painted a pitiful picture for our young minds of conditions in Africa, wherever that was, and we gladly parted with the occasional copper. On the short timber counter, there was a mite-box with a little statue of a kneeling black man on top. When a coin was dropped in the slot, the head of the statue nodded back and forth. 'You see,' Annie would say, 'the little black baby is thanking you.' It was a miracle! Of course, much later on we learned that we could retain Annie's goodwill by tipping the head of the statue with one finger while her back was turned for a moment!

With my penny at the ready, I asked Annie for a pennyworth of the ten-a-penny sweets. She asked me if I had made my First Confession. I proudly assured her that I had. She told me that this was a big day in my life, that God was so good to me, that I was now full of God's grace and that I shouldn't forget to pray for the 'black babies', and maybe even give a little something to ease their starvation. Being so full of goodwill after my confession, and with a desire to remain in Annie's good books, I had no choice but to share my penny with Annie's 'black babies'. I changed my order to a ha'penny worth of the sweets, settling for five sweets rather than ten. However, she gave me the extra one which removed some of the pain of my charitable act. Hoping that the little black man would appreciate the great sacrifice I had made, I dropped the ha'penny through the little slot. The little black man vigorously nodded his thanks! Annie beamed at me. I was in her good books!

Munching happily on one of my sweets, I started to walk towards home, feeling very pleased with myself. As I left the edge of the village I heard the clip-clop of a pony and the sound of iron-shod wheels coming behind me. It was a pony and trap. 'Jump in and take your feet off the road,' a harsh voice grated at me. It was a command rather than an invitation, a command in a voice that brooked no argument. I obeyed with alacrity! When Lizzie Bawn told you to jump, you jumped without question. The nickname 'Bawn' was a total contradiction. She always dressed in black, with a black cap covering her head and her ears. Her dark complexion and her equally dark hands gave a distinct impression that soap was not one of her major household expenditures. She was well known for her bad temper, while her rapier-sharp tongue ensured that nobody wanted to become involved in an argument with her. She lived a short distance from the school, near the small glen where we sometimes went to pick sloes. We were careful not to go near her house as she always carried an ash-plant which she would not hesitate to use on any trespasser. Some of the big boys in school told us that she was a witch and that she had a collection of empty coffins in a shed near her house, ready to be put to use if any of us went too near the house, and we believed every word! Her husband, a carpenter, had died several years earlier. He also had been the local undertaker. She lived alone on her small farm of three or four cows and, in all probability, had a very lonely existence, a fact which would not be understood by young children who were more than a little afraid of her.

I hastened to obey her instruction to 'jump in'. Anyway the Missus had often warned us about the sin of disobeying our elders and I had no intention of jeopardising the shining condition of my newly-cleansed soul by disobeying Lizzie Bawn! 'Close the door of the trap after you. There's a breeze on my feet,' she growled at me. I closed the small door behind me, twisting the piece of cord around the nail that was there for that purpose, the lock having long since disappeared. Her fat figure took up most of the right-hand seat. A girl from my First Confession class, Nellie, was seated in the left-hand side. Nellie was a big girl, much bigger than any of us, and had a large mop of fuzzy hair. She was a tomboy, played football with the boys and was well able to use her fists if an argument started. I sat down beside her on the narrow seat. Lizzie Bawn picked up a frayed plaid car-rug with fringed ends and spread it over our laps. 'Tuck that in around your knees,' she instructed, 'and keep out the breeze. Did you tell all your sins to the priest?' she asked. I told her I did. It was the first time I had been in her pony and trap. 'G'wan! G'wan,' she shouted at the pony. We left the village behind us as we began to move towards home. Lizzie took a small round box of Hignett's snuff from the pocket of her apron and, holding a pinch between her fingers, she inhaled a few loud sniffs. I hated the smell of snuff. Lizzie seemed to spill more down the front of her coat than she had inhaled. She sneezed twice, shaking the trap. 'The Lord have mercy on the dead,' she intoned. We responded with a reverent 'Amen'. The story of the coffins in her shed flashed through my mind, but today of all days I was not going to entertain any bad thoughts about anybody! I was determined to be extra good and to become a more responsible person!

After driving along for a short distance, I felt a sharp rap on my left ankle. I jumped a little, but concluded that it was only an accidental kick from somebody's shoe. However, after a second and then a third kick, I abandoned the accident theory. A sharp elbow to the ribs followed by a pinch on my leg under the cover of the rug, convinced me that this was deliberate intimidation. I looked at Nellie. She had a lovely innocent look on her face as she conversed sweetly with her neighbour, Lizzie Bawn. While I fidgeted to get away from her bony elbow and pinching fingers, she turned and gave me an angelic smile and continued chattering away with Lizzie. But the seat was too short and the punishment to my ribs and legs continued. The last thing I wanted to do was attract Lizzie's attention because it was obvious that they were good friends and I would get no sympathy from her. My patience was running out very fast! I couldn't take much more of this carry-on!

My first reaction was for instant retaliation! Taking Nellie's size and strength into consideration, I knew that hand-to-hand combat was out of the question. I might get one or two 'licks' to my credit in a surprise attack, but disaster would soon catch up with me. I suddenly remembered that I had just completed my First Confession and here I was, planning mayhem already! I recalled the words of the Missus, telling us about the devil roaming around the world, trying to tempt people to commit sin and put big black spots on their souls. There and then, I had this terrible feeling that all the little red devils in Hell were sitting there in Lizzie's trap, urging me to give Nellie at least one good 'clatter' of my fist! The Missus had also told us that God would test the sincerity of our goodness, but I felt that He was getting a little over-enthusiastic in my own particular case and that a much easier test would have been sufficient. I clenched my fists tightly under the rug and fought back the temptation. The elbows to the ribs and the ankle-tapping continued unabated. Lizzie glanced across at me a few times and said, with a frown, 'You're a very fidgety young lad, aren't you?' Easy for her to talk! She didn't know what I was putting up with.

Even though God had once said something about 'turning the other cheek', I was not totally convinced that He had taken Nellie into consideration. I craftily thought of a solution to my problems – bribery! With a forced show of goodwill and generosity, I pulled out the small brown paper *tóisín* containing my three remaining sweets from my pocket. With feigned magnanimity, I offered them to Lizzie Bawn and Nellie, harbouring a slim hope that my offer would be turned down, especially by Lizzie who was toothless, and the sweets being of the rock-hard variety. No such luck! 'Thanks,' she grunted as she daintily picked a sweet from the *tóisín*, studied it for a moment and popped it into her mouth. But Nellie, with a wicked glint in her eye and a sweet smile on her face, shoved her pudgy fingers into the *tóisín* and, before I realised what was happening, grabbed my two remaining sweets and put one of them into her mouth. I was left holding the empty *tóisín*. I began to hope that it would go with her breath but stopped the thought in mid-air when I remembered that any 'bad thought' would also put a spot on my soul. I was paying a terrible price for my state of grace, and the faster I got home the better!

I could see the cross-roads approaching. I was almost home. Nellie had left me alone and had neither pinched nor kicked me for the past few hundred yards. Maybe she had seen the error of her ways and had decided to refrain from trying to draw the wrath of Lizzie Bawn on my head. I was sure that God had come to realise how good I really was, despite all the tribulations I had to endure. Even though my dignity and pride were badly bruised, I was not going to be forced by Nellie into retaliation – well, at least not until after my First Communion. A rough outline of a plan was forming in my mind and I realised that having made my First Communion I would have a whole month to get my revenge on Nellie before my next Confession came along! I had no doubt but that the priest would understand any drastic measures I might have to take from Monday onwards. After all, the pinching and the kicking would try the patience of a saint, but as for her taking the last two sweets I had in the world, that was the last straw!

Just as I was putting the final touches to my plans, I got an unmerciful pinch in the side of my leg. Having been lulled into a false sense of security, I jumped a foot off the seat with a scream of pain and rage. I gave Nellie a good shove as she looked at me in a wide-eyed gaze of injured innocence. 'Did you see what he did to me and I not doing a thing to him?' she shouted at Lizzie Bawn. 'I did indeed, love,' retorted Lizzie, and she turned towards me, swinging her ash-plant and whacking me across the knees with it. The plaid rug took some of the sting from the blow, but still I felt it. 'Leave that little girl alone, you little ruffian you,' she roared as she swung the stick again. I waited no longer! Throwing the rug to one side and caution to the winds, I took a massive leap out of the trap, without taking the time to open the rickety door. I heard the swish of the stick behind me, but she missed. Too late, I realised that the ground was a long way down. I landed with a thud on all fours on the road, scraping both my knees and cutting my hand on the rough surface.

Gingerly picking myself up, I saw the triumphant smirk on Nellie's face as she waved a derisive goodbye to me from the departing trap. Lizzie Bawn turned back in the seat, as though nothing had happened, and shouted at me, 'Tell your Mother I'll be up to her in a week or two with a hatching hen for her.' I was about to tell her what she should do with the hatching hen but I controlled my outburst. Dear Lord, what more do you want to throw at me? It had been a bad half-hour! Father O' would not be too pleased with the thoughts of vengeance that were flashing through my mind if he were here right now! Looking down, I surveyed my new scratches and cuts and viewed with dismay the mud and dust that clung to my clothes. How could I go home looking like this? There was a drain, half-filled with running water, beside the road. With the help of a few broad dock-leaves dipped in the water, I washed off, as best I could, my bloodied cuts and cleaned away most of the mud. I was not able to do a great job but it might pass a casual inspection. I could hardly believe what had happened in the past half-hour. The Missus had never told us that it was so difficult to stay in the state of grace. But my rage was slowly evaporating and everything was returning to normal. In fact, I was becoming inwardly very pleased with myself that I had survived all my temptations – well, almost!

CHAPTER 6

The Main Course Is Bacon!

In the 1940s, choosing the meat for dinner was never a problem. The vegetables may have changed seasonally but bacon, in its many guises, was always on the menu. The only ceremonial deviations were the goose at Christmas and Easter and, occasionally during the year, the chicken or more truthfully the hen, especially on 11 November, St Martin's Day, as custom demanded the spilling of the blood of a fowl in honour of St Martin, for some obscure reason now lost in the mists of time. The occasional piece of 'fresh meat' was brought home on fair days, provided the cattle had been sold. Boiling mutton or beef were favourites, closely followed by steak or chops. The wonderful smell of frying steak would fill the kitchen and be wafted out the open door to assail the nostrils of passers-by on the road. I suspect many of them often used the excuse to balance their bicycles against the front wall of the house and call in to say hello to my mother. It seemed that the big kettle in our house was never off the boil and whatever meal was on the table was shared with the unexpected but always welcome visitors. The occasional treats of 'fresh meat' were always treasured, because we knew that tomorrow it would be bacon again.

Every house killed at least one pig each year, depending

on the size of the family. With only Mother, Father and myself, one pig was more than sufficient. This major event usually took place in October or November when the weather was cooler and flies posed no threat. But the killing of the pig was only the climax of a long, well-planned process. The choosing of the pig was all-important. I often listened to my father as he chatted with a neighbour while making his choice. It was like a race-horse trainer deciding that a foal, because of certain characteristics, would be a future Derby winner. This early spring choosing of the ideal pig followed a time-honoured routine. The pig was examined from all angles. The length of his snout, the straightness and length of his back, the firmness and curve of his shoulder were all taken into account and the final decision was not taken lightly.

Following this selection process, the Chosen One must surely have noticed a marked improvement in the quality of his life. He was immediately placed in regal isolation where traditionally the woman of the house looked after his feeding and fattening. He was treated with great care, getting large portions of boiled potatoes, 'Indian meal' or maize, crushed oats, pulped vegetables and creamery milk. Getting the pig to the peak of condition was an art in itself. An overfat pig produced very fat bacon, often referred to as 'daub' which, I might add, was highly prized in some households but not in ours. Killing a thin or under-fattened pig was not alone unprofitable and unproductive, but could also have repercussions on the honour and good name of the household. Some people might even be bad-minded enough to think that there was a shortage in the house if that family couldn't wait long enough to fatten the pig properly! At the creamery – the great rural forum of the forties and fifties – a pig killing would be discussed on the following morning among the groups of farmers while they awaited the arrival of the manager in his pony and trap from Cree. As well as being an economic necessity, going to the creamery was a daily social occasion at which the local 'characters' amused their fellow-suppliers with anecdotes and amusing comments on recent happenings. The news of the killing of a thin pig was a challenge the 'characters' couldn't resist as they tried to outdo each other in humorous comments about the unfortunate pig. Somebody would start the ball rolling by saying that he heard the late lamented pig was 'a little bit on the thin side'. The comments would come fast and furious – 'Wisha God help us, he was like a rasher with a pig's head at one end', or 'That bacon will move fast, sure he was a greyhound of a pig to start off with.'

My father loved all animals with very few exceptions. The pig was one. He hated them, but he loved bacon, so a compromise was reached and the bacon won. The small shed adjoining a half-acre paddock was always assigned to the reigning pig. That was the fattening pig's territory, but woe betide all concerned if the pig pushed open the little gate and got in to the nearby calves' field. The 'prayers' that descended on the head of the adventurous pig seemed to impress even the pig as he would run squealing back to his own sanctuary. Father kept the shed spotlessly clean with fresh bedding every day, but beyond that both he and the pig went their separate ways. Mother fed the pig and I felt that she was the real judge of when the pig was ready.

At least a week before the pig would be killed, a fixed plan of operations would swing into motion. Each of my parents had their own preparations to make. Mother would gather all the necessary ingredients for her own particular recipe for the black puddings, enlist the help of a couple of her friends and assemble the collection of pots and pans. My father took care of the rest. His first assignment was to go off on his bicycle to engage the services of Paddy the Butcher, who lived about three miles away on the other side of the village. He was acknowledged as the best pig-butcher in the area, most humane and with a perfect record for curing bacon. His marvellous skills were often explained away by locals as being the result of spending years in America – which seemed to explain everything. I remember him as a big, jolly, ruddy-faced man who spoke with a slight American accent or an 'American slang' as we called it. He travelled about on his bicycle with a bag containing the tools of his trade, tools which both fascinated and terrified me as a child. He neither received nor expected any money for doing this work. Instead, he would take home a generous portion of meat and, later on, my father would give him a day's work, cutting turf or saving hay. As a child, I reasoned that I should always endeavour to stay in his good books, seeing what he could do to a pig!

Having been promised the services of Paddy the Butcher for a particular day, my father drove the pony and trap the fourteen miles to Kilrush to buy the big bag of salt that would be required. The days before the big event were filled with boiling kettles of water to wash and shine a host of white enamel buckets and basins until they were dazzling. The big tub, or 'kief', and the meat barrel were scrubbed and washed until they too shone. The big shed, the 'car-house', got a massive spring cleaning. All cobwebs and dust were brushed from the ceiling, the flagged floor was scrubbed with buckets of boiling water, broken windows were repaired or boarded up and the bottom of the large sliding door was checked for any gaps to ensure that the cat would not get in.

On those days, I learned to make myself as scarce as possible as I seemed to get in everybody's way. I also had no desire to see the pig. With my awesome knowledge of the exact day that Paddy the Butcher was due to arrive, I felt I could not look the creature in the eye in case I would blurt out the dreadful information. His beady, glaring eyes seemed to bore directly into my childish soul. I found other places to play. The further I got from the pig, the less were my feelings of guilt.

I never liked the day before. The usual happy-go-lucky atmosphere of the house was disrupted. There was so much work to be done with all the final preparations. From early morning, the normal rhythm of the household was accelerated beyond recognition. Nobody had time to answer the stream of questions I wanted to ask. My mother told me to 'Run out and play', while my father told me to 'Go inside and maybe you can help Mother with something.' It was a long day and everybody was tense.

One of the last jobs to be done was to fill the two big water barrels standing by the back door with fresh spring water. It would all be needed the following day. By the time one barrel was full, our own well at the rear of the house was getting very low. Father would then have to draw the water, two buckets at a time, from a neighbour's well down the road at the bottom of the hill. Anxious to help, I would march beside him, swinging my little tin can, which had originally held Cleeves toffees. Since I was not allowed near any well because of 'the big black dog below in the well that would eat you up in one gulp', my father filled my can first, then his own bucket, and we walked proudly up the hill, side by side, two men doing their work. By the third trip, the hill had become very steep, the can of water was getting heavier and heavier, the wire handle was inching deeper into my fingers and cutting a white furrow across them even though I kept changing hands, both shoes were now over-flowing from the splashing water and, anyway, that barrel was never going to be full. Secretly grateful, I allowed my father to persuade me to take a rest!

We passed by the pig's paddock each time on our way to the neighbour's well. Sometimes the pig would be rootling with his snout in the paddock, other times he would be standing at the gate, grunting at us as we passed. I didn't like pigs. They were very unfriendly to six-year-old boys. One couldn't play with them or pat them like a horse or a dog. Believe me, I had tried hard to be friends with this particular pig. I had tried talking to him and I had tried rubbing him through the bars of the gate, only to have my hand almost snapped off for my efforts. Truthfully, only I wouldn't dare admit it, I was terrified of that big hairy monster whose huge jaws seemed to go slurp! slurp! all day and who, I was convinced, would consider a six-year-old boy a rare delicacy. As I walked up and down the hill past the pig, making sure to keep my father between the pig and myself, I recovered my bravery and my voice and I certainly told that pig my opinion of him. My father appeared to enjoy my bravado and explained to me that, despite what I thought, pigs were God's creatures too. But I couldn't believe that this ugly, unfriendly, bad-tempered, sloppy brute, could be connected in any way with the same God who made all the other lovely animals. Or maybe God just made a mistake and now we were stuck with it. However, tomorrow would fix all that.

I woke the following morning to the low hum of conversation. My small room lay directly off the kitchen. The cows had been milked, the calves fed, the milk-tank was ready for the creamery, and now they were having their well-earned chat over breakfast. Waking up in the morning to silence in the house was always a little disconcerting – perhaps this was part and parcel of being an only child. But the murmur of conversation in the kitchen in the early morning always gave me a happy, warm feeling. It was so reassuring – all was right in the world. I snuggled deeper under the blanket and, with the help of a vivid imagination, enjoyed my boyhood day-dreams for a further half-hour.

Suddenly I returned to reality with the realisation that the big day had arrived, the day on which my arch-enemy, that grumpy pig, the bane of my life, would get his come-uppance. I charged into the kitchen, full of boyish energy, and an-nounced to Dad that I was going to help him kill that pig. He chided me quietly for my blood-thirstiness, sat me on his knee and reminded me that I liked animals and that an animal should never be killed except from necessity. He often said things like that to me though at the time I had no idea what they meant except that they appeared to be sobering thoughts, a damper on my enthusiasm.

By mid-morning the tempo of activity had reached a feverish pitch. The huge open fire was piled high with turf, my Mother red-faced from working close to it. The big black metal pots of spring water were hung on the crane and swung inwards over the blazing fire. When the water boiled, that pot was lifted to one side, to be replaced with another. I sensed the tension in my father as he made the final preparations. Youth has its own built-in antennae for such feelings and I made sure not to cross him in any way.

Considering the harsh economic conditions of those war years, the killing of a pig was an important day in the life of a small farmer. If something went wrong with the butchering or the preserving, it could spell economic disaster. Having to purchase an already fattened pig at the market or fair could easily cripple him financially for the rest of the year, possibly until the small creamery cheques began to arrive the follow-ing summer. But such weighty matters would be beyond the comprehension of a six-year-old!

I felt myself drawn to walk by the pig-pen to have a quick

look and, perhaps, to gloat over my old enemy. He seemed quite unmoved by all the excitement. He still glared malevolently at me and gave me a warning grunt. However, as the morning wore on, his time became shorter and shorter and I became a little unsure of myself. Enthusiasm was waning rapidly. When I heard Dad say to my mother that it was time to move the big kitchen table out to the car-house, things were becoming very ominous. The more I thought about this matter, the more the pig's personality improved. Maybe he wasn't as bad as I made him out to be; maybe I should have tried harder to make friends with him; maybe he couldn't help being cranky and bad-tempered; maybe he had a bad tooth or a belly-ache and wasn't able to tell us; maybe Dad was killing him because I was always saying that I was afraid of him and that I disliked him so much. By the time Paddy the Butcher arrived on his bicycle and was having a cup of tea, I really liked that pig, while at the same time my liking for the friendly Paddy was on a definite downturn. Why did he have to keep his promise and be so punctual? If only he had got a puncture or even broken the chain of his bicycle on his way to our house, maybe Dad would have changed his mind and there would be no need to kill my friend the pig!

A few of our close neighbours arrived to help, my uncle Jim, Michael from next-door, and Pat, who had a moustache and smoked a pipe. I loved watching him clean his pipe with a *tráithnín*, or piece of rush, then cut the plug of tobacco with a wicked-looking white-handled penknife, knead it between his hands and fill the pipe. After tea, he would light the pipe with a red ember from the fire and puff away contentedly. 'A good honest man' my father always called him, his highest accolade. The conversation around the table continued for a while, the great events of the day − compulsory tillage, the war, the scarcity of goods. I was lulled into a false sense of security, my misgivings forgotten, until my father announced that 'We may as well make a start, in the name of God.'

The reins from the horse's winkers was picked up from outside the door. They would be placed on the pig's leg to walk him up the road to the car-house. At this point my courage failed me and I ran, crying, up the road to our neighbour Eileen, who was like a grown-up sister to me. Not being able to see and hear was, at least, a small consolation. My unmanly tears were a temporary embarrassment, but she understood and didn't make fun of me. Some time later, after peering out the small gate in front of her house, she told me it was safe to go home if I wanted to. I trotted home rather sheepishly, but nobody seemed to have noticed my hour of weakness.

Fortunately during my absence the pig-blood had been taken away in the big white pans and the carcass was now lying on the table. Curiosity was beginning to overcome my previous fears and self-recriminations, even though I still declined several offers to touch the pig to make sure he was dead. He may have been dead to them but I preferred to wait a little longer to be doubly sure.

My father looked very relieved and was his old self again. The world was becoming a better place already. The big timber 'kief' was filled with boiling water from the kitchen. Small saucepans were used to pour the hot water on the carcass to soften the bristles. Razor-sharp knives, held with both hands, were dragged against the grain of the bristles, shaving away the stubble until the skin was perfectly smooth. It was hard work. The men perspired freely in the steamy dankness of the car-house. Buckets of boiling water arrived at a steady pace from the kitchen. Streams of warm water flowed out the car-house door and into the drain outside. Sitting on my heels on the verge of the drain, I launched an armada of leaves and bits of stick which became mighty warships and liners on a great ocean, with a few torpedoes thrown in for good measure to account for the many shipwrecks.

By the time I tired of playing with my flotilla of ships, great progress had been made in the car-house. The carcass had now been cut open. Paddy the Butcher tried to initiate me in the basics of biology by showing me the pig's heart, but, with heaving stomach, I declined. More washing followed and eventually the whole thing was wiped dry with white linen cloths. A ladder was propped against the wall and the carcass was hung upside down from the top rung with a rope around the hind trotters. Three clean sticks were prepared, about eighteen inches long and pointed with Pat's sharp penknife at both ends. The long slit down the underside of the pig was pushed open and the sticks were inserted at intervals to keep the cavity in this open position. A sheet of white muslin was draped around the carcass to exclude dust and to discourage any wandering fly. Everything was washed and brushed clean – the floor, the table and the fearsome butchering tools.

I still refused all requests to put my hand on the pig, but when the men went into the kitchen to have their well-earned meal, I ventured to approach the carcass and touch it with one finger. Nothing happened, no frightening grunt, no gnash of teeth. This was no longer a pig, it was just bacon. It was hard to associate the animal I dreaded with the smooth skinned, headless carcass on the ladder with its shiny purple-pink rib-cage visible through the long slit down the middle. I remembered having seen something similar hanging in a butcher's shop window in Kilrush. I was no longer afraid. I gave it a good punch in the side to show my disdain. But I could still remember when it was alive and there was no way I wanted to eat any of it. However, seeing that it was now so harmless, I left the final decision open, just in case I should change my mind.

My father always gave the pig's head to Corney the Blacksmith, an old friend of his who lived about a mile up the road. Corney was one of the best-liked 'characters' in the area. I remember him as a big elderly man with a very bushy moustache, a large briar pipe and always wearing a big black hat. He was a fanatical card player and his house beside the forge was a favourite haunt for the locals going on *'cuairt'* – often he had as many as ten visitors a night. The deck of cards was always produced and small 'penny gambles' took place there almost every night. Corney was an exceptionally honest man and played cards strictly by the rulebook. God help anyone he caught tricking, renaging from the trump card or giving 'tokens' to their partners – the deck would be gathered up, the house cleared and the oil lamp quenched!

No sooner would the pig's head be delivered than Corney would spread the good word of a big tournament for that same night with an entrance fee suitable to the occasion, perhaps three pence or even six pence per player. If Corney was not satisfied with the turn-out, he split the pig's head down the middle and thus made two nights out of it, thereby ensuring two nights' entertainment for himself and, of course, a few shillings to boot.

The day after the pig was killed was a day of contrasts in our house. My father seemed very happy and contented that all had gone well and went about his normal day's work, taking pains to keep away from the kitchen as much as possible. And for good reason! From mid-morning onwards the kitchen was a scene of organised bedlam. This was 'filling the black puddings day'. Mother had centre-stage all to herself and she had enlisted the help of two friends. Only the narrower entrails were used, or 'covers' as mother euphemistically called them. And then the washing began! It seemed to go on forever. They were washed, turned inside out and washed again. They were cut into two-foot or three-foot lengths and the washing process began again. Eventually, Mother was satisfied.

Next began the gory business of filling the puddings. The blood was strained into a huge white enamel basin. She had her own recipe which she followed to the letter. Everything was measured – the oat meal, the chopped suet, the onions and a whole plethora of spices which she kept in little glass jars on the top shelf of the glasscase. It looked terrible! I decided that all the chatting and laughing was designed to keep their minds off the awful-looking mess! Each length of pudding was firmly tied at one end, leaving about a foot of twine hanging loose.

Filling the pudding was a very tricky business. First of all, the covers were very slippery, a fact that caused several mishaps and much enjoyment and laughter. Secondly, the average tin funnel that one could buy from a travelling tinsmith had sharp edges and would puncture the puddings. Experience had shown that the best funnel was the glass globe from the kitchen lamp, with its narrow chimney and wide base. The narrow end was inserted in the open end of the cover and the mixture was slowly poured in. Care was taken that it was free of air-bubbles and that it was not packed too tightly as this would lead to many burst puddings and, after all, a housewife's reputation was on the line. About three inches of space was left at the top to allow for expansion before being tied securely with the loose twine from the other end, creating a great loop of pudding with about a six-inch gap between the two ends.

While all this work was taking place, the big black iron pot was simmering over the fire. At last the filling was completed and the white basins were piled with the unsightly, unappetising loops of pink-grey puddings. They were ready for the final stage of the process. A clean rounded stick was placed across the mouth of the black pot. Several loops of pudding were hung from the stick with only the twine protruding above the simmering water. They were allowed to cook for some time. Then the stick was lifted up carefully and the suspended loops inspected. They were now a dark brown colour and a lovely appetising aroma filled the kitchen. To allow them to cool slowly, they were hung from a long pole which was balanced between two tables in the spare room. They should be ready for frying tonight!

By mid-afternoon the work was finished and the women had gone home. It was evident that Mother had enjoyed the companionship of the two neighbours for a few hours. The work was made lighter by the laughter and storytelling. I couldn't follow most of their jokes, but I was happy that they were happy and I laughed when they laughed. With the kitchen returned to normal, Dad was soon back in his favourite chair by the fire, tilted backwards on its back legs against the wall. Enjoying a cup of tea before the evening chores began, Mother regaled him with the stories she had heard. Some of them had whispered endings that were not for my ears while others contained words that were spelt out, letter by letter. I hated this. It always spoiled what might have been a good story!

Tonight, Paddy the Butcher and Michael from next door would be back to salt the bacon and put it in the meat-barrel. The kitchen lamp, a double-burner with two wicks and a polished reflector behind the globe, was filled with paraffin. The pot-bellied glass globe, having survived its temporary job as a funnel, was washed in suds and polished until it glistened. The wicks were trimmed carefully with the scissors, cut straight across the top and the corners rounded so that they wouldn't 'smoke' and blacken the globe. The tall brass single-burner standing lamp from the parlour got the same treatment. The extra light would be needed tonight. Father built a low stand with pieces of timber in the corner of the car-house, on which the meat-barrel would be placed. The barrel itself had been scrubbed and polished and was ready. I invented a new game with the barrel. Leaning over the verge and shouting into it, my voice was amplified greatly. I talked, shouted and sang bits of songs until I was hoarse.

Other preparations continued though on a more muted scale than the previous day. Mother reminded Dad that a light would be needed in the car-house later on. My father had two territories which were his undisputed domain and to which trespass was strictly forbidden – the press under the glasscase for hammers, pincers, nails and so on, and the garret or attic over the two smaller rooms off the kitchen. Up there, Father stored larger items – his 'thrumpery'. He placed one of the strong kitchen chairs against the partition and stood on it. Reaching up, he opened outward the partially concealed door of the garret and pulled down the broad-stepped 'stairs'. Climbing up to the garret was strictly off-limits for me. I had been warned about another 'big black dog' up there! However I had already come to the conclusion that this particular 'black dog' had fooled Dad and perhaps had slipped out the small garret window in the gable of the house some dark night. I would surely have heard him walking around up there because my bedroom was underneath. On the other hand, maybe he was able to come and go at will so it certainly wasn't worth taking a chance. Dad climbed into the garret and re-appeared with the tall storm lantern with the thick glass globe and the long wire handle. So that was where he kept it, and I had searched high and low for it. It was the ideal toy for playing 'trains' because the guard of the train had to have such a lantern to give signals to the driver. I immediately started adding up the pros and cons of risking a visit to the garret. It must be like Aladdin's cave up there, a treasury of interesting items. It seemed hopeless at the moment, but some day I would get there! Having replaced the ladder and closed the garret door on my temptations, Dad proceeded to clean the smoky glass globe, and pushing it upwards on its wire frame he pushed a length of precious candle into its holder on the base, closed down the glove and it was ready for lighting later on.

At about eight o'clock, Paddy the Butcher arrived on his bicycle. Opening the door, he greeeted us with the usual 'God bless all here', to which we all answered 'And to you too.' Fresh tea was made, a sod or two added to the fire, and the neighbourly good-humoured talking started. There was no thought of sleep on my mind. This was a special night and I was allowed to stay up. The talking seemed to go on forever. I had to fight hard to keep my eyes open in case I was packed off to bed. At last the *seanchas* formalities came to an end and the men reluctantly dragged themselves away from the blazing fire.

The kitchen table was lifted from its usual place by the wall and put in the middle of the floor. The big bag of salt, which had been keeping dry near the fire, was lifted on to a chair close to one end of the table. The carcass was carried in from the car-house and Paddy set about carving it into three lengthy sections, the two sides or flanks and the long backbone. Paddy's great black-handled knife flashed wickedly in the lamplight as he began expertly to cut away large strips of porksteak. The pile of steak in the white basin, held by my father, grew rapidly. Then the backbone and some other bones were cut into pot-sized portions, ready for cooking or roasting over the next few days.

With that much out of the way and everything tidied once more, the salting began. A full side of bacon was laid flat on the table. The hind quarter, or ham, was cut off and very lightly salted. This was wrapped in muslin and then parcelled with twine. It was hung at the side of the fireplace, a little way up the chimney where it would become, in due course, a prized smoked ham to be used on special occasions. The remainder of the side of bacon was then cut into four or five manageable pieces, or 'flitches'. Using a very pointed knife, Paddy punctured the skin all over with tiny perforations. These would help the curing process. The salt was rubbed liberally into the meat until the table began to resemble a small snow-covered mountain. Language got a little rough at times if the salt pierced any little laceration in hands or fingers. And all the time the talking and yarning continued!

Paddy and Dad talked about the days they had spent in New York, New Jersey and Chicago. They exchanged stories about the great St Patrick's Day parades, about prohibition and 'moonshine', about the big Crash of '29 and its resultant poverty and unemployment. Strange placenames from another world floated about the kitchen – the Bronx, Brooklyn, Manhattan, Van Nostrand Avenue, Amsterdam Avenue, Ellis Island. I had heard some of those names before, and they sounded strange but fascinating. I tried to visualise what those places were like. I had been to Kilrush a few times and I thought that was BIG. When Paddy explained that New York was as big as the distance from our house to Kilrush, all of fifteen miles, I knew that such a place was an impossibility. I felt that it would sink into the ground with all that weight and that with so many streets and houses, people would always be lost and never able to find their way home!

While I was wrestling with these imponderables, they had

finished salting all the flitches of bacon and stacked them in the meat-barrel in the car-house until the barrel was almost full. A wet blanket was placed over the mouth. This would create humid air inside the barrel, thus drawing the moisture from the bacon. The resultant liquid became brine because of the salt and it was this brine that preserved or cured the bacon. Some timber boards were placed on top of the barrel, with a heavy stone to hold them in place and, at the same time, discourage any inquisitive visits from the cat or from Teddy or Fred, the two dogs.

The work was finished and the car-house door closed tight with a peg of timber wedged in the hasp. The kitchen was cleaned and brought back to normal. A feast was being prepared as the men pulled up chairs at one side of the fire, giving Mother plenty of space to do her cooking. The fruits of their labours were about to be tasted. Red coals were pulled out from the middle of the fire, the three-legged 'brand', or stand, was placed over them, with the big iron frying pan sitting on top. Soon, pieces of porksteak were sizzling in the pan, followed by inch-thick rings of black pudding. The smell was wonderful! All eyes followed Mother's every movement from the fire to the table and back again. With feigned reluctance the men allowed themselves to be coaxed to the table. There were a few muttered standard statements such as: 'Yarrah! Alice, you shouldn't have gone to all that bother. Shure the plain cup of tea would have done fine.' My father took the first taste of the porksteak and, looking around the table, he wished everybody *'Go mbeirimid beo ag an am seo arís'* – may we all be alive and well this time next year.

The years have not dimmed the memory of how wonderful that porksteak tasted. It was magnificent, from the crispy outside to the succulent inside. In later years, I have often wondered what gave those steaks their great flavour. Was it the freshness of the meat or was it the slow frying in the iron pan over the red coals? After that regal feast, my eyes were refusing to stay open and I was grateful to be sent off to bed. As I drifted to sleep, I could hear the sound of happy voices from the kitchen, a lot of laughs and a few verses of a song from Michael, who was a lovely singer. I can still hear him singing 'My Little Grey Home in the West', 'The Old House' and 'Boolavogue'.

On the following day, the tradition was to share our new-found fortune with neighbours and friends. A portion of steak and a loop of black pudding were wrapped in greaseproof 'butter-paper', perhaps from eight to twelve parcels in all. Distributing the parcels with my father was one of my favourite jobs, as one was assured of a warm welcome in each house. I sat on the cross-bar of his bicycle, and we set off on our journey with a laden straw message-bag swinging from the handlebars. We were received at every house with offers of a cup of tea or a bottle of stout for Dad. He graciously refused most of the offers as one or two glasses of stout was his limit. However, I accepted all that was offered to me. I gorged myself on glasses of lemonade, orange squash and biscuits – the big Geary currant biscuits, or 'currany cakes' as they were more popularly known. During the pig-killing season, usually from the end of September to Christmas, each house would slaughter a pig so we, in turn, would receive similar parcels.

The bacon stayed in the barrel of brine for at least three weeks and sometimes up to five weeks, depending on how salty the household liked their meat. The longer in the barrel, the saltier the bacon. When they were taken from the barrel, the flitches of cured bacon were hung in the kitchen, probably serving a three-fold purpose – for convenience, for display and for further curing from the heat of the kitchen. A thick beam of timber, usually about four inches by three inches, stretched across the kitchen. It was firmly anchored to the rafters, about a foot above the top of the side walls. Strong meat-hooks were attached to the beam and the flitches, wrapped in paper and tied with twine, were hung from the hooks. In some houses they were left uncovered. A well filled meat-beam was a source of great satisfaction and an indication of a certain affluence. The pig was killed, the bacon was cured, the pit of potatoes was at the back of the house and plenty of turnips and cabbage were growing in the kitchen garden. We were well prepared for the approaching winter!

In the late forties, the traditional kitchen became the first victim of modernisation. The rural electrification scheme was in its infancy. The hitherto bare rafters and collar-braces with their insulating layer of dried sods were being covered with ceiling boards or panelled with sheets of plywood. In many cases, the intrusive meat-beam was removed forever. An interim solution was a long board bolted to the top of the kitchen wall from which the flitches were hung. The hanging bacon was no longer the eye-catching centrepiece of the kitchen. It was the beginning of the end of a way of life. Within the space of a short generation, dramatic changes took place. The urban butcher slowly replaced people like Paddy. Pigs were being killed in factories rather than car-houses or sheds. The turkey replaced the Christmas goose. Innocence became an endangered species. Even the horse was replaced by the tractor. Part of traditional rural Ireland died with the arrival of the boarded ceiling and the electric light!

CHAPTER 7

Farm Friends

To survive and raise a family on a small farm during the years of World War II was a constant uphill struggle. The average farm produced most of the food for the table and tried to make enough money to purchase the essentials that could not be grown or made on the farm. Just 'making ends meet' was an achievement and a source of contentment. Surplus money was an almost unheard of and unusual luxury. Ground rent and rates were the only annual outgoings that were not directly associated with food production, household goods or clothing. There were four basic elements in this finely-balanced art of survival – the family, the farming skills, the neighbours and the farm animals. Living so close to nature, people got to know each of their animals individually, especially their eccentricities. Each of our cows had a pet name, bestowed on them by virtue of their colouring or derived from the name of a previous owner. We had Polly, Daisy, Grogan, the Roan, Speckled, Big Red, Small Red, Handlebars and Murphy. Each cow had her own place in the milking shed and any one of them who rashly sneaked into another's place to steal a mouthful of hay was quickly pucked back to her own territory.

My father always told me that with cows I should be 'firm but kind'. The kind part was fairly easy but the firm gave me endless trouble. I never could master it, mainly because the cows refused to take me seriously. When collecting the cows for evening milking, Dad would open the gate on the Clune road and shout, 'Come on, girls. How! How!' Every one of them would cease grazing, amble up to the gate and walk quietly home. It was so easy! Some evenings, I was sent to drive them home. I could shout 'Come on, girls' until I was hoarse for all the good it did me. The cows just looked up and continued grazing, totally ignoring my assumed authority. Eventually I had to run back and forth, to the point of exhaustion, chasing each cow individually through the gate. Even on the way home along the Clune road, they stopped every few yards to grab a mouthful of grass from the side of the road as though they hadn't eaten for a week!

I have always felt that each particular cow has her own personality. There are leaders, followers and rebels. These can be sub-divided into gentle cows and aggressive cows, even-tempered and bad-tempered, calm and highly strung, and ranging from fairly clever to plain stupid. Every herd, however small, seems to have a natural leader who makes decisions for the others. When driven into a field, the leader will walk to a particular area and the others will follow. Should there be a strange object, such as a fluttering piece of cloth, on the side of the road that frightens the cows, the leader will approach it very carefully, examine it for a moment and, having satisfied herself that it doesn't represent danger, will lead the others past it with no further problems. But, as with humans, there are always one or two cows who decide things for themselves and do things their own way. They will not turn in a gate with the others but will walk maybe fifty yards past it, stand and wait to be collected and driven back to the gate, usually with some 'sweet prayers' heaped on their uncaring heads. Such cows are never leaders though they may have some bovine ambitions in that direction.

In our small herd, Polly was the undisputed leader. She was smaller than the others but was the only one without horns which, to me, made her look different, like a man with a receding hairline. She was a pet who seemed to enjoy human company. I could always approach each cow and would be allowed to rub her sleek coat, but Polly had that extra touch. If I held out my hand to her, she would lick it just like a dog. She would then lower her head and allow me to scratch behind her ears, something that seemed to please her very much. She had a daughter in the herd, and actually, several years later when her muzzle was turning grey, a grand-daughter joined her in the milking shed.

However, Polly and I had our ups-and-downs, especially on a few occasions when I had been despatched to drive the cows home. There was one very puddly gap between two fields where I had to skirt around the verges to keep my feet dry. The other cows would trundle their way through the mud, but now and again Polly probably felt like playing games with me. She would stand smack in the middle of the mud, looking back over her shoulder at me. No amount of pleading, cajoling, threatening or shouting would budge her. She just stood there, probably laughing at my futile efforts to get her to move and to keep my feet dry at the same time. Eventually there was nothing left for me to do except walk through the squelchy mud and drive her out. And, every time, no sooner had I taken a few steps into the mud, sinking half-way up to my shins in the sticky mess, than Polly walked sedately out the other end, looking back at me as though she were saying, 'Fooled you again, didn't I?' I was convinced that Polly had a sense of humour as black as her sleek coat!

The young calves were very quiet and friendly and loved to be rubbed and petted while they were housed in their shed during the winter and spring months. But once the weather became warm and mild, they were turned out into their field – and very reluctant they were to leave their warm, familiar shed. They had to be shoo'd and pushed and sometimes even lifted across the yard to the gate of the field. There they would stand in a huddle, nervously surveying their new surroundings. Eventually one of the braver ones would take a few tentative steps further into the field, closely followed by the others. After a few minutes, they walked another couple of yards on the unaccustomed carpet of grass. One could actually feel their fears being replaced by an increasing confidence. Suddenly they realised that they were free and their exuberance knew no bounds. They raced madly around the field, kicking their heels in the air. They gambolled and chased each other like little puppies until they were exhausted and out of breath. After some time, instinct took over and they began to nibble at the lush grass.

Every morning and evening they came to the gate to be given a warm drink of boiled maize porridge mixed with creamery milk. Mealtimes were a little unruly as each one tried to gulp down his own portion as quickly as possible before trying to steal his neighbour's as well. They licked their buckets dry, head-butting them in an effort to extract more. The head-butting habit sometimes had hilarious results, especially if the handle of the bucket slipped over the calf's head. Suddenly realising that somehow or other the bucket had become attached to his head the poor animal panicked immediately and he would race around the field as though every dog in the parish were chasing him, until eventually he got rid of the offending bucket. The calf never came to any harm, which is more than could be said for the galvanised bucket. Learning from experience, I always made certain to keep the handle of the bucket under the calf's chin to avoid such calamities.

After about two days of their new-found freedom the calves lost their tameness and returned to the wild. They no longer wanted to be rubbed or petted. They were no longer playmates!

We had two dogs that were total opposites of each other in every respect. Each went his own way and, seemingly by mutual agreement, completely ignored the existence of the other. If dogs could talk, I doubt that they would have been on speaking terms, even though they never had a fight. Fred was a big, friendly, shaggy sheepdog with an aversion to work. He stayed close to the house, spending most fine days relaxing on top of the grassy ditch across the road from the front of the house, watching the world go by but not willing to play an active role. On wet days, he adjourned to the haybarn to continue his observations. To justify his existence, he always went with my father, morning and evening, to drive home the cows. He slept in the haybarn and was a good watchdog, barking loudly at any intruder, be it fox or human – it is quite probable that he barked in irritation at his sleep being disturbed rather than through any sense of duty. He loved human company and was a good friend and playmate for me for many years.

On the other hand, Teddy was a small black-and-white Pom of questionable ancestry. He was arrogant, peevish, bad-tempered, and was suspicious of everybody, strangers and neighbours alike. But he was a one-man dog. He gave unswerving loyalty to my father, following him everywhere. He was well trained and obeyed every command my father gave him, but totally ignored orders from anybody else including Mother and myself. If Dad left some object, a coat, a fork or a shovel, lying in a field, he would say to Teddy,

'Mind that', and may God help anyone who came near that object. He would protect it, all day if necessary, until my father came back to retrieve it. Teddy rode with Dad in the horse and cart around the fields and even went to the turf-bog with him, seven miles away, sitting beside him on top of a load of turf on the way home. The only other farm animal he tolerated or showed any affection for, was the horse Grey Fann. They seemed to enjoy a great rapport. Any outsider who approached Grey Fann, even to stroke her, would be given a warning snarl by Teddy who would take his stand in between Grey Fann's massive hooves, ready to defend his friend until such time as Dad told him to 'sit'.

On one particular day, Teddy was sunning himself on the big, square, stone flag outside the front door while Fred was in his usual spot, on top of the wall across the road. Two stray dogs came along, trotting peacefully down the road and minding their own business. Teddy immediately decided to defend his territory and show the two strangers that he was the boss. He leapt out on to the road, teeth bared and barking furiously. The two took offence at this unprovoked black-and-white nuisance. They launched a two-pronged attack. Fred watched the fracas with ears erect for a minute before concluding that Teddy had bitten off much more than he had bargained for and was getting the worst of matters – his aggressive barking had quickly changed to high-pitched yelps. Fred jumped off the wall and into the swirling mass of fighting fur. Within a matter of seconds, the fight was over, with the two strays running down the road whimpering, their tails between their legs. Teddy picked himself off the ground, body trembling, the hair standing upright on his back with rage and indignation.With flashing teeth, he snapped at Fred's fluffy side as though he was saying, 'I didn't need any help from you, you big oaf. Couldn't you see I had the two of them beaten on my own?' Fred just looked down at him and calmly returned to the top of the wall as though nothing had happened. Teddy went back to the front door to lick away the pains of his battle. About half-an-hour later, I saw Teddy cross the road and sit on top of the wall beside Fred. They sat there side by side, facing in opposite directions and staring haughtily into the distance. It was one of the rare occasions that Teddy and Fred sat quietly beside each other as dogs usually do. They stayed on top of the wall for several hours. By the following morning, I noticed that normality had returned and both Teddy and Fred were once more going their separate ways.

CHAPTER 8

The End of the Summer Holidays

On the first Sunday in September the kitchen was full. All the neighbours had gathered to listen to the wireless. The reception was crystal clear. To the left of the wireless, the red dry-battery looked very new. On the right, the arrow-shaped needle on the side of the glass wet-battery showed that it was fully charged. The golden voice of Michael O'Hehir filled the packed kitchen and spilled out through the open window and door to the few on the outside who couldn't find room inside. The All-Ireland hurling final was being played in Croke Park between Cork and Dublin. Our part of Clare on the west coast was a football area and very few had seen a hurling match, and even fewer had been to Croke Park. Yet, through the voice of Michael, Croke Park was as familiar as our own backyard, and the hurling heroes of Cork – Christy Ring, Jack Lynch, Bat Thornhill, the Lottys, the Youngs and the Murphys – were household names to us all. There were even a few in that crowded kitchen who proudly proclaimed that they were well acquainted with relatives of Michael O'Hehir who lived about fifteen miles away in the townland of Paradise on the banks of the Shannon. It gave everyone a sense of familiarity with the great commentator.

Later that evening, in the quietness of our own yard, with

a rag ball and a piece of a stick, I tried to emulate the artistry of Christy Ring while giving a running commentary on the imaginary proceedings, using many of Michael's well-known phrases like 'the clash of the ash' or 'a schmozzle on the verge of the square'. It was a memorable afternoon for all his listeners, dispelling their cares for a few brief hours with his vivid word-pictures of the pageantry and excitement of the game.

But, for me at least, that glorious day was overshadowed by a looming dark cloud. On that first Sunday in September, the last Sunday of the summer holidays, Father O' dashed all our hopes of a last-minute reprieve when he announced at Mass that all the schools in the parish would re-open the following day. Preparations had been under way for over a week. I had got a new schoolbag, blue canvas with red trim around the edges. The shoulder straps were fastened at the front with two silvery hooks. With growing apprehension, I thumbed through my new books, recognising immediately that they were much more difficult than my old books and had a host of big words. Mother covered each one with brown paper and my name was written carefully on the front. On the one hand I was looking forward to returning to school as I would have so many playmates, most of whom I would not have seen since the beginning of the holidays. But on the other hand the prospect of the classroom and the drudgery of learning was not appealing. However, I felt that the fun in the school yard more than made up for the trials and tribulations of the classroom!

Monday morning dawned bright and sunny, an ideal day for playing around the yard or the haybarn. During breakfast I was issued with a litany of instructions about my conduct in school: 'Don't forget your manners', 'Be respectful to the Missus', 'Don't be bold', 'No fighting, arguing or pelting stones', 'Don't get your shoes wet', 'Come straight home after school' and 'Don't lose the cork of your milk-bottle'. In those pre-screwcap days, bottle corks were a very scarce commodity. Most kitchens had a big jam-pot in a glasscase in which corks of all sizes were hoarded. Corks were very fragile and had to be handled gently. Sometimes, despite the best of care, the cork broke. The remaining portion in the neck of the bottle had then to be pushed into the bottle and fished out with a loop of twine. In the absence of a proper cork, a tightly-rolled paper 'cork' was a poor replacement because it leaked so badly. Therefore, losing the cork of one's milk-bottle at school could have dire consequences!

The new schoolbag was given a final check. The books were all in place, the Irish reader, the English reader, a headline copy, a sum copy, a catechism and, the bane of our lives, a tablebook. In the small pocket at the front of the bag was a new timber pencil case containing a pencil and a wooden-handled pen with the nib reversed in its holder to prevent it getting 'crossed'. Mother had prepared my lunch, a few slices of bread with plenty of butter and a sprinkling of sugar – a treat for my sweet tooth! A bottle of milk completed my lunch menu.

I was ready! The schoolbag was on my back with the shoulder straps hooked across my chest. Dad was drinking tea at the table, having completed the morning chores. The summer had been great fun but had passed so quickly. Why did it have to end so abruptly on this beautiful sunny morning? I said my goodbyes to everyone, including Fred the sheepdog. Teddy, the small dog, ignored me as usual and pointedly looked the other way. I got spattered from head to toe with holy water as Mother liberally wielded the quill from the bottle at the front door. One final look at the familiar surroundings and I was on my way down the dusty road, keeping well in by the ditch as I had been warned. There was no traffic on the road except for the few stragglers returning from the creamery. They all shouted encouragement to me as we passed each other: ''Tis fine for you, off to school for yourself', or else 'You'll get no slaps today from the Missus, it's only your first day back!' I found neither greeting very uplifting! I trudged slowly down the hill and across the valley, stopping for a moment to locate the position of a lark who was singing his heart out in the blue sky overhead. How free he was – no worries about school, the Missus, tablebooks or being incarcerated for the nicest part of the day!

After almost a mile of solitary contemplation, I met a few more classmates who seemed equally despondent. A little further along the road, at the Kilkee cross, we joined a larger group of nine or ten. Within moments, the air of gloom had disappeared. We were soon chatting and laughing. All too quickly, we reached the school gate. The place looked cleaner and tidier than when we had left it in early July. We had poured through that same gate, singing in raucous chorus, 'Six weeks and a fistful of sweets.' On the last day of the school year, the Missus always divided a tin can of sweets between her charges. But that was a long six weeks ago and now we were back again. Father O' had got Jamesie to whitewash the walls. The door and the window frames had been given a fresh coat of dark green paint. The old puddly corner of the school yard was dry and had a light covering of short grass. It would soon be worn down by running feet. We just had time for one game of tag, or 'tig' as we called it, before the Master came out and rang the bell.

We filed through the Master's room and into the inside room where the Missus awaited our arrival. She seemed very happy to see us again. Maybe I had misjudged her after all! Following our promotion from high infants, my class was now seated in the centre of the room with the second class to our right and the infant classes to our left. She told me to sit in the front seat. Not a great location at all! I was now seated in front of her desk, directly under her eyes, with nowhere to hide! I shared the double desk with Paddy, who lived to the west of the school, beside the sea. At least for the coming year I was rid of Nellie with whom I had shared a desk last year and who had tormented me on my First Confession day. She was bigger than any of us, packed a terrific punch, was very bossy and never stopped talking in class! At least twice last year, the Missus had slapped me hard across the fingers with her rattan cane for talking in class, all because Nellie had complained that it was I who had been asking her questions when in fact I hadn't opened my mouth!

The Missus was fussing with the infants, especially the new 'low infants' who were starting school for the first time. From our new exalted position in first class, we could easily develop an air of superiority over mere infants, especially the few who cried and kept asking to go home. Paddy drew my attention to one particular 'cry baby' in the back seat who appeared to be sobbing uncontrollably – but not a tear had dampened his eye. After a whispered discussion, we both agreed that the new boy was over-playing his act and that the Missus would sort him out very quickly. She spent a long time with the infants and eventually got them interested in playing with the *márla*, the soft play-putty, and with the *cipíní*, the long matchsticks. The crying stopped and now they seemed very happy to be in school. We had no objection to all this attention being given to the infants as it meant she didn't have time to be bothering us!

But our period of relaxation was short-lived. She wrote a headline on the blackboard in her beautiful script and instructed us to take out our headline copies and copy it down 'in our best handwriting'. Pens were carefully dipped in the little white ink-wells in the front of our desks and we applied ourselves to our writing. Our concentration was rivetted on the red and blue lines of our copies, tongues moving like the pendulum of a metronome as we struggled to copy the headline, letter by letter. What had looked rather simple was now becoming very complex! Obviously, the long summer lay-off had not helped our penmanship. It was extremely difficult to keep the individual letters exactly inside the two blue lines. The nibs seemed to have developed a mind of their own! What did the Missus keep saying? – 'The top of the "f" and the "l" touch the upper red line; the bottom loop of the "f" and the "g" touch the bottom red line, but the upstroke of the "t" does not go as far as the top line!' It was all very confusing. The end result was a squiggly ink-splattered disaster. She was not pleased! She warned us sternly that we would go back to doing lines of individual letters until our writing improved. As she cleaned the blackboard, we clearly heard her say to herself that she was surprised that a few of us had been promoted in the first place and that she would have to think more about it before it was too late! We looked furtively at each other, wondering whom she had in mind.

A knock on the door brought a welcome interruption. The new Master came in to call the rolls. Many of my fellow-pupils were seeing him for the first time and busily assessing him, wondering if he would be 'easy' or 'hard'. I knew him quite well as he had come to live during the summer in the Master's residence, which made him a next-door neighbour of ours. On several occasions, I had casually mentioned to my classmates that the new Master and myself were very close friends. Catching his eye, I gave him a big smile. But he didn't seem to notice. He seemed to look straight through me as he surveyed the classroom. Opening the big roll book, he read out our names, all in Irish. On hearing our name, we each answered with a loud 'Anseo'. He read my name. I shouted confirmation of my presence. Not a flicker of recognition crossed his face! I was having second thoughts about the new Master. Was this the same friendly good-humoured man who called so often to our house for a chat with Mother and Dad? Was this the same person who had climbed over the fence on so many occasions to help Dad save the hay in the meadows? Today I was seeing him in a different light and, quite frankly, I was a little disappointed in him, especially as I foresaw some awkward questions coming my way at lunchtime in the school yard. I studied his face as he finished calling the rolls. He had the same stern look on his face as the Missus, very serious and unsmiling! Sometimes grown-ups can become very complex and unpredictable.

At last the short midmorning playtime arrived. I was starving and wolfed down one slice of bread and butter. There was a buzz of conversation as we discussed the morning developments. The noise got louder and more shrill as we chased each other around the yard. Somebody produced a rag ball, tied up with twine, and a game of football was quickly organised with rolled-up coats for goalposts. Within minutes, the first argument had developed – did the ball go inside or outside the 'goal post' or even over it? Further hostilities were averted by the Master ringing the bell. We trooped back to the classroom, red-faced and breathless from our exertions.

It was time for the tablebooks! Instead of the terms addition, subtraction, division and multiplication, we had our own names for them – the 'and', 'from', 'into' and 'times' tables. This year, we would be doing only the 'and' and 'from' tables, and they were quite a handful for one year. It was bad enough trying to memorise them or shout them out in class, but then the Missus asked us questions at random, mixing the sequence of figures and causing us countless problems as we mentally raced down through that particular table to reach the right answer. We spent some time repeating the tables aloud in a sing-song chorus. At home Mother taught me my tables, but now and again Dad decided without warning to examine me, and he was even tougher than the Missus if I made an error. I came to the conclusion that the easiest and safest way out of this problem was to memorise the tables until I knew them backwards. After some time, the Missus wrote small sums on the blackboard which we dutifully copied into our sum-copies. We struggled to find the correct answers as quickly as possible. Even though I wouldn't dare admit it to my classmates, I enjoyed doing the sums. But the Missus still gave me a tongue-lashing because my figures and the neatness of my sum-copy fell far below her high standards.

At last, at last, it was time for lunch. The slices of bread were devoured in record time. One of the other boys dropped and broke his bottle of milk but each of us gave him one 'slug' out of our own bottles to make up for his loss. We were still a little hungry but we were racing against the clock. We quickly re-started our game of football which, we all felt, had been quite unnecessarily interrupted by almost two hours of school work. Warnings at home about kicking stones or scuffing our boots and shoes were quickly forgotten in the heat of the game. Our lack of skill did not diminish the excitement as we kicked the rag ball up and down the yard with wild abandon, sometimes connecting with the ball, though more often kicking the shins of opponents. Knees and palms were soon covered in mud, but there was running water in the ditch across the road with plenty of grass to scrape away the dirt and hands could be rubbed dry on the seat of one's pants! The strident ringing of the bell restored peace and tranquillity to the school yard where the new grass in the puddly corner was already looking the worse for wear. One last glance upwards at the cloud-flecked blue sky and we surrendered ourselves to the mysteries of education.

The afternoon passed in a series of highs and lows with most of the classes seeming to pass very quickly while one or two seemed to drag on forever. I loved the English spelling, the reading and the arithmetic, while the catechism was often interesting especially when the Missus told us some of her lovely stories. The Irish classes created problems for me, but not for the usual reasons. I often became bored after a few minutes of the endless repetition of small words and lost interest in what the Missus was saying, lapses for which I often paid dearly. Actually I was still unaware of the huge headstart and advantage I had over my classmates. My Granny, my father's mother, stayed with us for long periods each year. She was a lovely gentle lady with a soft musical voice who always seemed to have a few sweets in some pocket of her apron. She spoke beautiful clear Irish as it had been her mother-tongue when she was growing up in what was one of the last Gaeltacht areas in Clare. I grew up speaking both languages though I didn't recognise them as two separate languages. To me at that young age, I simply talked differently to my Granny than I did to other people. We always conversed in Irish, even long before I started school. She had a wonderful stock of stories, some of them about kings and princes and great warriors, which could go on for days. It probably was for those reasons that my mind often wandered during those early Irish classes with the Missus. My thoughts strayed to home, wondering what Dad was doing right now – was he working with Grey Fann, and was Fred the sheepdog was lonely while I was in school?

And so our first day back in school came to an end. We shouted out our evening prayers with renewed enthusiasm and wished the Missus a heart-felt '*Slán leat*' as we left the room in single file. All semblance of order disappeared on reaching the school gate, as we romped, jumped and skipped our way along the dusty road, delighted with our sudden release from 'captivity'. I had plenty of company as far as the Kilkee cross but was again on my own for the final mile. I ran most of the way. Grey Fann was in the yard so Dad must be in the kitchen having a cup of tea. I burst in the door, full of news and stories of the day. Even Fred was delighted to see me, putting his front paws on my shoulders and licking my face. Teddy turned his head away, ignoring me, but I noticed that he too was wagging his tail. I poured out all my news of the day. They seemed to enjoy my opinion of the new Master, especially the fact that he appeared to become a totally different person when he was in school. While it was of no immediate concern to those of us in the Missus's room, it was still too early to establish if he would be 'easy' or 'hard'! In fact, time proved him to be a wonderful under-standing teacher who, despite our best efforts to the contrary, provided all of us with an excellent education and gave us a good foundation for life.

Many years later, his predecessor who had been principal when I first went to school and joined the low infants class, told a story against himself but of which I had no recollection whatsoever. He was unmarried at the time and lived the life of a happy bachelor in the Master's residence near our house. On a particular Monday evening as he locked the school door his best friend, also a teacher, called for a chat. The friend was one of the few who had a car, though how he managed to get petrol was another story. I was given a lift home and was put sitting in the back seat. It appears they both had been to a dance on the previous night and now wished to discuss their mixed fortunes of a romantic nature. In fact they wanted to talk about girls! Because of my presence in the back seat, they switched to speaking in Irish. Halfway home, the former Master recalled that he turned to his friend and said, 'Why the hell are we trying to talk in Irish? That little fecker in the back seat has better Irish than myself!'

CHAPTER 9

Preparing for Winter

Preparation for the Christmas season didn't begin on Christmas Eve or even a week before. In different ways, the preparations began in the late spring and early summer. In some ways it reminded me of Mother knitting a multicoloured pullover. There were many coloured threads hanging from differently shaped pieces of knitting. It seemed an incomprehensible tangle of unrelated bits and pieces. Then, one night, with the deft use of a needle and thread, she puts all the pieces of the jig-saw together, ending with one completed garment. It was like a magic trick! Christmas was like that. There were numerous unrelated threads or happenings that wended their separate ways from mid-summer onwards, until by Christmas Eve they had woven themselves into the season of joy, happiness and thanksgiving that is Christmas. 'God' and 'family' were the key words in the Christmas season of those boyhood days. Commercialism had not yet arrived in west Clare and was still a long way off.

By mid-summer the pig was being fattened and the geese were already getting the occasional extra ration of boiled potatoes and crushed oats. Work on the land continued at a hectic pace, saving the hay, filling the haybarn, or, on a damp summer day, putting the red turf creel on the horse-cart and going to the bog, six miles away, for a load of turf. It was a long journey for Dad and Grey Fann. Three creels of turf were considered a good day's work, though two would be the average. Each load was dumped or 'heeled up' at the back of the house. Later on when the cows were milked and the other chores completed, my father began the foundations of the long turf-reek, 'clamping' the longer sods of turf on top of each other to form the outer shell of the reek, the sods tilted outwards so that the winter rains would trickle down to the ground on the outside rather than penetrate to the interior of the reek. Because of the long journeys to the bog, bringing home the winter's fire was a slow process, but in a tree-less area such as ours turf was the only available fuel. Once the hay was completed, Dad concentrated on the turf until the great high reek was completed. Then, with his swinging scythe, the long green rushes were cut down and tied in sheaves. With these bundles, he thatched the reek with a thick layer of rushes, tying it firmly in place with a network of cord and *súgán* ropes, ensuring its protection against the wind and rain of the approaching winter. We were assured of a roaring turf fire for Christmas!

With the days getting shorter, it was time to dig out the potatoes and harvest the turnip crop. Picking the potatoes was a back-breaking job. In fact, two 'pickings' were done on each row. All the medium-sized and large potatoes were picked first, the bucket being moved along the newly-dug drill until it was full, before being emptied into the horse cart on the headland. These were destined for the table, although some would be retained for seed for the following spring.The rejects, or small potatoes, were then picked and dumped in a separate heap. They would be boiled and fed to the hens, the geese, and the fattening pig over the coming months. When my father's back was turned, many of those small potatoes were pushed back into the earth with the heel of the boot to avoid further abuse to an aching back and to frozen mud-caked fingers that kept dropping the tiny potatoes before they reached the bucket. But it was hard to fool him! Sometimes he strolled down the newly-cleared row behind me, scratching the loose surface with the four-pronged fork and resurrecting the recently buried miserable little potatoes from their early graves! Quite casually he would remark, 'You seem to have overlooked a few of them.' He had either been very lucky or else he knew more tricks about picking potatoes than I had heard!

The potatoes were carted home and piled in a long heap in the sheltered kitchen garden at the rear of the house. They were allowed to dry thoroughly in the soft autumn breezes for a day or two before being covered. But every crow, jackdaw and magpie for miles around must have heard the news of the uncovered potatoes in our kitchen garden. They arrived in droves for a free meal. However, they hadn't taken Teddy, the small dog, into account. Bad-tempered at the best of times, he really surpassed himself on this occasion. He sat near the potatoes and dared any of the flying raiders to come down and attempt to steal one. They perched on the trees and bushes, chattering and cawing in anger and frustration. Feathers flew when one crow swooped too low over Teddy in an effort to scare him. The bird was lucky to get back up in the tree where he surveyed the damage and regretted his brashness. The battle of wits continued from dawn until dusk. Teddy seemed to be enjoying himself, walking away slowly from the heap of potatoes only to turn sharply and race back, barking furiously at some foolish magpie or crow who thought their luck had changed.

After being allowed to dry for a day or two, the potatoes were covered with a blanket of dried rushes. The potato pit was completed by digging a drain around the long heap and shovelling the black earth over the heap until it was completely covered. The sides were then tamped down with the back of the shovel, thus ensuring that the long, black, smooth-sided pyramid would withstand all kinds of weather. A similar pit was made close by for the turnip crop. On the other side of the kitchen garden was a good-sized cabbage patch where the sturdy York plants would give a good supply of fresh cabbage throughout the winter months. The vegetable larder was now established and would have an important role in the Christmas preparations.

From early November onwards, the importance of the postman reached an exalted plateau in the everyday lives of our rural community. He was the 'bearer of good tidings', in fact the only link with far-off family members and relatives. He brought the Christmas card and the longed-for letter. The first postman, or 'postboy' as they were called, that I can remember was Whistling Paddy. He lived in the distant town and cycled over thirty miles a day on his heavy black bicycle with a wide metal carrier on the front and another at the back. He was famous for his happy whistling and always had a cheerful word for everyone. He came to know everybody's relatives and knew when a letter was due. Should an expected letter not arrive from a son or daughter in America or England, he often reassured a worried old lady, 'I have no letter today for you but don't worry, I'll have one tomorrow!'

In those dark troubled years of the thirties and forties the survival of many households depended on the arrival of the postman with the all-important letter which had a cheque or money order from departed family members. They made sacrifices in their adopted land in order to be able to send home the badly-needed pounds or dollars. Of equal importance was the American parcel, which usually contained much-needed articles of clothing with a few grocery items hidden in the folds of the clothes to avoid the attention of customs. The arrival of such a parcel was a welcome blessing and a source of joy to the entire household. Despite the war being waged in the Atlantic, some parcels still got through, although it took several months in some cases. In the weeks before Christmas, it was a source of wonder and awe to all how Whistling Paddy managed to cycle on his laden bicycle. He was a Santa Claus on two wheels, coming daily instead of just one night. Both the front and rear carriers were stacked high with mailbags and cardboard boxes and, as Whistling Paddy approached along the road, all one could see of him was the shiny peak of his postman's hat as he peered over the mountain of mail in front of him. He was a welcome guest in every house and the kettle was always singing over the fire should he like a cup of tea. Paddy knew everybody and he knew most of their private business, but he gained the respect of all because he never gossiped or 'carried stories' from one house to another.

We were less fortunate than many of our neighbours in that we never got more than one small parcel at Christmastime. One of Dad's sisters in America, despite having a large family of her own, always sent a few things in a parcel. Many items of used clothing came, but most welcomed were the few grocery items – a couple of pounds of currants and raisins, a pound of tea, some coffee for Dad, a glass jar of sweets, a tin of pears, a pack or two of cigarettes which had gone musty and a tin of powdered mustard which delighted Mother, as it was impossible to get during the war. I had never seen mustard until then but I learned quickly to avoid it after my neighbour, Eileen, tricked me into eating a spoonful, having told me it was a new brand of custard! The arrival of the currants and raisins guaranteed us a Christmas cake, and we had a little celebration to mark the arrival of the parcel. The items of clothing were examined and admired, some of the sweets were eaten and Dad made a pot of coffee.

During the early days of December, Mother would decide to whitewash the outside of the house if the weather was suitable. The lime was slaked, the long-fibre whitewash brushes were put steeping overnight in a bucket of water and a blue-bag was dissolved in a two-pound glass jam-pot filled with water. Mother donned the oldest clothes she could find, which was just as well because within a half-hour, she was covered from head to toe in whitewash spatters. I loved to help but I always appeared to get more whitewash on the ground, on myself and on poor Fred than I got on the wall itself. Dad got the long ladders from the haybarn and white-washed the gables and chimneys. He never liked painting or whitewashing. After the outside was completed, Mother decided, 'while she was in the humour', that the kitchen needed a 'rub' as well, especially over the mantelpiece and the two hobs at either side of the fireplace. Afterwards the flagged floor was scrubbed and washed with buckets of warm water. I never liked that particular part as it took hours for the stone flags to dry and, of course, my running in and out was curtailed mainly because I had to clean and thoroughly dry my shoes before entering the kitchen. I found it easier to stay outside until the floor had fully dried. When it was dry, the chairs and table were put back in place and I was happy to see everything coming back to normal. But not yet! The smoke-stained strip of oilcloth hanging from the mantelpiece shelf was pulled down and burned. The tea-caddy, the big clock, a tray and some china figurines were taken from the shelf and cleaned. A new white strip of oilcloth with a floral design and a moitred edge was tacked on to the shelf. The big picture of the Sacred Heart was lifted down from its nail on the wall and given a thorough cleaning and polishing. The small brass Sacred Heart lamp with its tiny red globe was polished until it shone. The kitchen was no place to be when Mother began her cleaning blitz! By the time she had finished, the house was transformed, looking lovely and bright with the fresh healthy smell of lime around the place.

Dad had become infected with the whitewashing bug also and decided to 'throw a few licks of whitewash' on the shed and the walls around the yard, all of which gave Mother a pleasant surprise. It gave the cows an even bigger surprise that same evening when, for at least five minutes, they refused to enter the freshly whitewashed shed, milling about in the yard probably wondering what had happened to their old familiar cowhouse! On the following day, Dad, in his newly acquired desire to help Mother with domestic affairs, decided that the chimney needed cleaning and that the ideal time to do it was when she had gone to the village on her bicycle to do her shopping. The long ladders were lashed together so as to reach the top of the chimney. Michael, our neighbour, climbed on to the roof and dropped one end of a long rope down the wide chimney. Dad tied a thick bundle of whitethorn branches to the middle of the rope. With Michael on top and Dad at the bottom of the chimney, they pulled the thorn bush up and down, up and down until the chimney was scrubbed clean. The bush had brought a cascade of powdery soot pouring down the chimney, enveloping Dad, the fireplace and half the kitchen in a cloud of fine black dust. He looked like the statue of the black man on top of the mite-box in Annie Fitz's sweet-shop! Looking at Michael through the haze of dust, Dad declared, in a gross understatement, 'Maybe we should have cleaned the chimney before she whitewashed the kitchen.' He gave the floor a quick sweep with the broom and seemed quite happy with his morning's work. Mother returned! It was most unusual for her to get really angry, but now she did! Dad rarely retreated, but now he did! He suddenly remembered some very pressing chores down in the fields and didn't come back for several hours. By then, much of the kitchen had been re-touched with the whitewash brush, the floor had been re-washed, dusting and polishing had been completed once again and Mother had forgotten her anger.

The day before Christmas Eve was busy. The plump goose had been killed. The flock of geese was by now decimated, as a few had been given to relatives and some to good friends, or 'well-wishers' as Mother preferred to call them. The goose for our own table had been plucked and the feathers were stored in a white cotton bag, destined for future use in cushions or pillows. The outer portions of both wings were put aside for later use as dusters or as an ash-brush to keep the hearth clean. After the plucking, the pin-feathers and down were 'singed off' over burning newspapers, leaving the carcass clean and smooth, ready for the next stage.

Christmas Eve was hectic! Dad had already picked a huge armful of ivy in the glen near the school. He carried it in from the car-house and dumped it on the kitchen floor. In this tree-less area near the sea, no holly grew and ivy was the only available evergreen substitute. The windows were decorated with long strands of ivy, with the Christmas cards displayed among the green leaves on the sill. A few strands of paper streamers, which were carefully stored from year to year, were strung across the kitchen and over the fireplace, and some short pieces were used in the windows. Mother produced a few glass jam-pots that had been stored in a cupboard. A big Christmas candle was placed in each one and sand was packed in, holding the candle firmly in position. A wide strip of coloured paper was wrapped around the jam-pot and tied with a piece of string. Local custom called for a candle in every window of the house, but we didn't have enough jam-pots for them all. I followed Dad to the turnip pit in the kitchen garden. In the pale wintery morning sun, the western slope of the pit was still covered in a white mantle of frost from the previous night. He opened the front of the pit and chose a few large turnips which he deemed suitable. With his pen-knife he cut away the tapering root to form a flat base. Back in the kitchen, he also cut away the tops and then, with the long blade of the knife, he cut a round deep hole in the top of the turnip and wedged the candle into it, making sure that it was firmly in place and wouldn't topple over. Some more coloured paper was tied around it and another window was ready.

Mother cycled to the church for midday Confessions, thereby leaving herself free to work all afternoon and evening in the kitchen. Potatoes had been boiled in the three-legged black pot over the open fire and had been allowed to cool. She now peeled and mashed them in the large white bowl. A plateful of finely-chopped onions was added, followed by plenty of butter and several other ingredients which she added from time to time until she was fully satisfied that the potato stuffing was exactly right. The carcass of the goose was stuffed and sewn up and then stored in the glasscase, ready for cooking on Christmas morning.

At that time of the year all the cows were dry except for one that supplied milk for the house. So, on Christmas Eve, all the chores were finished early in the evening, with each animal getting an extra ration of fodder just because it was Christmas. Before having supper, Dad took a bottle of holy water to the sheds and sprinkled some on all the stock and on the land. It was something he did twice a year, on Christmas Eve and on Easter Saturday. Then he boiled the small kettle of water over the fire and got ready to give himself an extra-close shave. The open razor, the 'cut-throat', was carefully honed on the strop which hung from a nail near the fireplace. He tested it, drawing it lengthways along a rib of hair and was satisfied. With the very hot water in the pan and a bar of red carbolic soap, and using his fingers only, he soon had a thick lather worked up. I loved to watch him shaving, noting every move and facial expression, all of which I tried to imitate. After each long careful stroke of the razor along his face, the collected lather was wiped off the blade on the edge of an old saucer that he had placed beside his adjustable shaving mirror. Strict silence was the house-rule while he was shaving. Any sudden distraction could be dangerous with that vicious-looking implement so close to one's face. I was really scared of that razor and nothing would get me to even touch it. He dressed in his best Sunday suit and a white collar and tie, all set to go to Confession. I kept admiring him, he looked so neat and well-dressed!

Before leaving the house, one very important Christmas tradition was fulfilled, the lighting of the Christmas candle. All the prepared candles were placed on the table. Being the youngest person in the house, I was lifted up to light the first candle. When it was lighting the three of us knelt on the flagged floor and said one decade of the Rosary. Taking the lighted candle in his hand, Dad took it into every room in the house, saying the brief Irish prayer in each room, 'Solas Dé orainn' – May the Light of God shine upon us. Returning to the kitchen table, the other candles were lit from the first one, before being placed in every window in the house. One had to check carefully that each candle was not too close to the curtain or the decorations. The tall brass oil lamp in the parlour was lit and placed in the centre of the table. The house seemed to come alive on Christmas Eve in the soft flickering glow of the candles, as I roamed from room to room, admiring the decorations and checking that the candles were burning evenly. We put on our coats and went outside in the cold night air to admire the lights from the outside. It was like a scene from one of the Christmas cards. As we came back into the kitchen again, I noticed that Dad had laid down the traditional welcoming carpet of green rushes at both the front and the back door. One could almost feel the festive spirit in the air. It was exhilarating — and Santa had yet to come!

On his way back from Confession, Dad called in for a minute to several of the neighbours to wish them a Happy Christmas. It was considered a lucky omen should a man call to wish a family a Happy Christmas on this particular night. Other neighbours called to our house and wished us the season's greetings. It was the season of goodwill! A drink was offered to each person and was rarely refused. It was going to be an early-to-bed night for me because all three of us were going to the first Mass at seven o'clock on Christmas morning. Of course, Santa would be arriving during the night, so getting to bed early was imperative! From a few comments I had heard at school, I harboured some grave doubts about the existence of the said gentleman, but I figured that silence was the better option for the moment, just to be on the safe side.

I crawled into bed, excited but tired. I watched for a while the flickering shadows cast by the candle in the window. The pale light gave the small room a very warm feeling. I must have fallen asleep within a few minutes because I didn't hear Mother come into the room to quench the candle.

CHAPTER 10

Christmas Day
Is Family Day

I awoke on Christmas morning well before six o'clock. It took an extreme effort to leave the warm cosy bed and walk across the cold floor. I welcomed the shouted invitation to dress myself near the blazing turf fire. The candles in the front windows were lighting again, totally disregarding the Government black-out regulations about showing a light in a window. In any case, what would a German plane be doing around west Clare on Christmas morning? We must have had a severe frost because I could see the icy patterns on the glass in the light of the candle. Suddenly I saw what Santa had brought me — a small red-and-blue football and a bag of sweets which nestled among the ivy leaves beside the candle in the window. Who could ask for more? However, I couldn't indulge myself until after Mass. In those days the very strict laws of fast forbade any food or drink from midnight before Communion. Knowing how much they loved their early-morning cup of tea, I knew this was a real sacrifice for Mother and Dad. Leaving the sweets untouched was my biggest problem!

Having made sure that all the candles were extinguished, the three of us began our mile-and-a-half walk to the village church for our Christmas Mass. It was bitterly cold and very dark, with millions of stars twinkling in the frosty sky. It was only when my eyes grew accustomed to the darkness that I became aware of the sheer beauty of the scene that surrounded me. Every window in every house held a lighted candle and, from our vantage point on top of the hill, the pinpoints of lights stretched for miles in all directions like a huge magic carpet. As we walked along the road, we played little guessing games, trying to identify the different sets of lights along the valley and on the sides of distant hills. The multitude of lights gave an indication of how thickly populated the area was at the time. It conveyed a feeling of belonging, of being part of a very big community.

We were joined by a few other families as we walked along. The women chatted together leading the group, while the men brought up the rearguard, a kind of voluntary segregation on grounds of common interests. Of course the aisles of the church were also segregated, with the women taking the right-hand row of seats and the men taking those on the left. A few horses and traps passed us on the road, each with the stump of a candle flickering in the lantern attached to the side of the trap. Everybody was so cheerful and friendly. Each person shouted the usual greeting, 'A happy Christmas to you,' to which we all replied in chorus, 'And the same to you and a great many of them.' When we reached the village, the street was lit up with the candle-light pouring from each window.

The church was packed with people from every corner of the parish. Many children vacated their seats to accommodate adults, and were seated on the step of the Communion rail, around the altar. Several hanging oil-lamps illuminated each of the three aisles of the church and the altar was an island of light. I felt that Heaven could not be a great deal more beautiful than this! The choir was quite close to where Dad and I were seated. The organist, Miss Tess, wore a big wide hat, with a long, coloured feather. I kept glancing at the feather, swaying back and forth, as she pumped the pedals of the wheezy old harmonium for all she was worth! Father O' began the ceremonies, assisted by a host of altar boys. I envied them in their black soutanes and crisp white surplices! I whispered to Dad that I wanted to be an altar boy. 'When you are a little bigger,' he said. That satisfied me! The heat of the crowd, the lights, the chorusing of the responses and the singing all had a very soothing effect on me, making me feel very drowsy. The lovely strains of the 'Adeste Fideles' at the end of Mass brought everybody to their feet as the whole congregation joined in the chorus of the final hymn.

We streamed from the church into the first light of dawn. The sun was peeping over the shoulder of Mount Callan as we walked through the village, stopping every few yards to shake hands with friends and exchange greetings. Several people insisted on giving me a few pennies for sweets, even though all the shops were closed. But there would be another day! A quick count of my finances revealed that I had become reasonably wealthy – I had a little over two shillings to my credit! The growing daylight showed us all the familiar houses and the frost-covered fields. The enchantment and mystique of the star-spangled darkness of our earlier journey had vanished with the dawn's early light.

It was good to get back home to the warm fire. This morning even our breakfast was a little different. With a very sharp knife, Dad had sliced some thin rashers from a lean flitch of bacon. Soon these were sizzling in the big iron frying pan, together with some eggs and several slices of homemade black pudding. One extra treat was a good slice of fried bread, a great favourite in our house. After breakfast I played with the new ball around the kitchen as the ground outside was

96

still frozen and a fall could be very unpleasant. Dad began reminiscing about Christmas when he was a boy in Cooraclare, several miles away. Listening to him recall his early boyhood days, with his older brother and four sisters, I felt very fortunate that conditions had improved so much in the intervening years. And most important of all, I had my Dad here in the kitchen with me. His father had died when he was only a baby!

On Christmas Day we would have no visitors nor would anyone be passing by on the road. It was a day reserved for one's own family, with everyone staying in their own home. It would have felt intrusive to visit a neighbour's house even on business. We had one very welcome exception and that was Michael, our next-door neighbour. He never smoked in the presence of his elderly father, even though the father knew for years that Michael loved his cigarette and had never objected or even passed a comment about smoking. What may have started as a gesture of respect for his non-smoking father, became a lifelong habit for Michael. He visited us several times on Christmas Day and again in the evening for a quick chat and an equally quick smoke. But in our house Michael was like a member of our own family. He was a good friend and a great neighbour.

After breakfast, Mother began the final preparations for cooking our Christmas dinner. There was a big fire in the hearth, with plenty of black turf to keep it stoked. The large lean ham, which had hung at the side of the chimney since Paddy the Butcher had killed the pig, was unwrapped and a generous portion was prepared for roasting. The two round, flat-bottomed, iron ovens, or bastibles as they were called in other parts of Ireland, had been scrubbed and polished and were ready for use, the large one for the goose and the smaller one for the smoked ham.

A bed of red embers was raked out from the centre of the fire and the three-legged 'brand', the pot stand, was placed on top. The stuffed goose was put in the oven with the required amount of rendered lard and spices. The oven was gently balanced on the 'brand' and the big iron lid was closed firmly. Using the long tongs, red-hot embers were piled on top. In similar fashion, the smaller oven with the ham was put at the side of the hearth. More black turf was added to the fire because a good supply of red embers was essential to the slow cooking. Later, the pot of potatoes and the skillet of vegetables were suspended from the crane over the big fire. Basting the goose and the ham from time to time was a very delicate operation. The ember-laden lids had to be lifted off cleanly but gently with the help of a small S-shaped pot-hook so that no ash or ember fell into the oven. A very steady hand was required for that particular job! After basting, fresh red embers were replaced both on the lids and under the ovens. My father always performed this operation, which had to be repeated several times. The tantalising aroma of the cooking filled the kitchen, arousing hunger pangs long before it was officially announced by Mother that our goose was cooked!

The dinner on Christmas Day was one of the rare occasions when Mother went 'all swanky' as she herself termed it. The new oilcloth on the kitchen table was covered with a white linen tablecloth. The special delph and cutlery from the parlour were placed on the table for the festive meal. From the top shelf of the glasscase, she took down the large willow-patterned serving platters, two of her most treasured possessions which had been in her family for generations. After the first course of homemade soup, the goose and the ham were removed from the ovens and put on the platters, ready for carving.

Memories of that particular dinner and of other Christmas

dinners of those bygone years are recalled with relish. They were not merely special dinners, they were festivals of food. No matter how harsh the times, no matter how great the scarcity of food, the Christmas table was a table of plenty! Perhaps it was the open turf fire or perhaps it was the slow cooking over the bed of red embers, but whatever the reason, the wonderful succulent taste of that Christmas goose could never be reproduced by even the most modern of electric gadgetry. My own particular favourite was the white meat and the potato stuffing. If my plate was filled with just those two delicacies, I would have been very satisfied. The helpings of roast ham, vegetables and potatoes added to the delight, making it the ultimate banquet.

I knew by the happy look on Mother's gentle face that she was justly proud of the dinner she had served and that everything had gone according to plan. Looking back, I feel we don't appreciate the cooking skills of those pre-electric days. The average modern home often has a shelf filled with cookery books and recipes and a kitchen filled with appliances, electric or gas cookers, microwave ovens, thermostats and thermometers, electric whisks and food processors. And all of this progress in one short generation! During those war years, every farmhouse had a big open fireplace on which everything was cooked, using a collection of different-sized cast-iron pots and pans. The one great skill developed by the housewife was that of 'eye judgement'. By the colour of the flame she could judge the proper temperature of the fire for a particular meat dish or for baking. She knew when a dish was cooked by a quick look into the pot.

Another great skill developed by the housewife was the art of 'fire management'. This was the ability to maintain the glowing embers and the fire itself, either under or around the different cooking pots, at a steady temperature, without any fluctuations. This may appear to be a very simple matter, but the quality of the turf was usually inconsistent, ranging from hard black turf to light brown or 'bran' turf. The blacker the turf the 'hotter' it burned. Unfortunately for the housewife, all the grades were mixed together in the turf-reek. She usually devised a system whereby she hand-picked the blacker turf for cooking and used the poorer quality 'bran' turf for stoking the fire at night when the family and any visitors sat around the hearth, talking and telling stories. Cooking the Christmas dinner in those years was not just a culinary achievement, it was a triumph over adversity!

CHAPTER 11

The Wren Dance

The wren, the wren, the king of all birds,
St Stephen's Day was caught in the furze,
Up with the kettle and down with the pan,
Give us our answer and let us be gone.

The dawning of St Stephen's Day marked the opening of the Christmas visiting season. After the traditional family gathering on Christmas Day, visits to relatives and neighbours were resumed once more. The bottles of stout were uncorked for the men, while the ladies enjoyed a discreet glass of port. One could feel the festive spirit in every kitchen and everybody was made welcome. It was a good time to 'patch up' minor differences which might have arisen during the year, such as trespassing cattle or problems with some right-of-way.

Most of the younger generation had been looking forward to St Stephen's Day for quite some time; they were planning to go out 'hunting the wren', or 'on the Wran' as it was commonly called. The anthem of the wrenboys, quoted above, was learned and rehearsed because it would be recited in chorus at each house that was visited. Some other song was also chosen, and practised for days beforehand. It was vital to know at least two verses, the first to be sung voluntarily while the second verse should be readily available should the listening household prove almost impossible to please before giving the wrenboys their hard-earned few pennies. Having prepared their musical programme, the next important step was to plan a route that would pay the highest dividend for the least amount of walking. The 'small Wrans', of two or three young boys or girls, rarely travelled more than a mile from home in any direction. Experience would have taught them the location of the 'good' houses and also the few where the reception might be less than enthusiastic. But even those latter houses would be visited in the faint hope that their generosity might have improved in the intervening twelve months. One other matter that had to be considered by the smaller boys was the danger, however rare, of being 'held up' by a group of bigger boys and forced to hand over whatever money they had collected. Even though this act of piracy was a rarity, the danger was always present, especially if the small boys ventured too far beyond their own neighbourhood.

On St Stephen's morning old clothes were donned, some people disguised their faces with boot polish, others wore funny masks, or 'eye fiddles' as they were called. Lots of ivy and coloured bits of paper were pinned to their clothing and each group carried a small bush, decorated with pieces of coloured streamers. I always envied the carefree young wrenboys who seemed to have such fun roaming from house to house, getting pennies for sweets and of course boasting later about all the money they had collected. However, my father refused point blank to allow me go on the Wran and no amount of cajoling would alter his decision. Sulking only made matters worse as I found out to my cost, so I accepted the situation!

The small wrenboys usually finished their 'rounds' in an hour or two, being quite satisfied if they collected a few shillings for sweets. Much more enterprising were the groups of adults who organised what were called the 'big Wrans'. Their primary purpose was to collect sufficient money to organise a big Wren Dance – a soirée, a night of dancing, eating, drinking, and revelry. Wren dances were arranged for any time between early January and Shrove Tuesday and could be held any night of the week except Saturday and Sunday nights. Saturday night was unsuitable because of early Masses on Sunday morning and Sunday night was inadvisable because dances in local parish halls were always held on Sunday nights, usually to raise funds for the parish. Any confrontation with a local parish priest spelled disaster for a Wren Dance! The women of each house, especially the single girls, were formally invited to the soirée, though the menfolk would be asked to 'donate' a shilling or two at the door on the night of the dance to help cover the extra cost of the refreshments that would be consumed.

On St Stephen's Day, the big Wran travelled from morning to dusk, moving many miles from home, walking, cycling, or even using horses and traps, or a combination of all three. A group of ten to twenty would include musicians, singers, step-dancers and set-dancers. They always gave value for money; the better the entertainment provided, the bigger the donation. All members of a big Wran disguised themselves at least partially. However, the big Wran from the local fishing village, famed for traditional music, was an exception to this tradition. They dressed in their 'Sunday best', their sole decoration being a red paper rosette in their lapels. They confined their entertainment programme to one step-dancer performing on the flagged kitchen floor to the music of a sole musician, reserving the best wine until the night of their big dance. A different member performed on the 'flag of the fire' in each house. The 'flag of the fire', in front of the hearth, was always the largest and smoothest in any kitchen. When dancing a Caledonian set or step-dancing a jig, a reel or a hornpipe, the best dancers usually chose the 'flag of the fire' to display their mastery of the intricate steps. Boots and shoes had leather soles and heels, and to protect them from wearing out too quickly a U-shaped iron 'tip' was nailed to the heel and the soles had rows of irons studs, hence the term 'hob-nailed' boots. The dancing of a set on a flagged kitchen floor was both a sight to behold and a sound to remember. The rapid tapping of the tips and studs would rise to a crescendo of rhythmic sound as the men tried to out-do each other in the art of heel-and-toe tapping, or 'battering' as it was called. Traditionally, an old iron pot or a bastible was placed under the 'flag of the fire' when it was being laid down. This gave it a certain hollow ring which amplified the 'battering' of the dancers. As the four couples dancing a set changed their positions during each section or 'figure' of a set, each couple had their moment of glory on the 'flag of the fire', giving the gentleman an opportunity to show his prowess at the 'batter-ing', to the shouts of encouragement from the onlookers. They cheered every display of skill and shouted unasked-for instruction such as, 'Wheel her, Pat!' or 'Round the house and mind the dresser!' The friendly rivalry between some of the dancers would be well-known to the crowd who never lost an opportunity to fan the flames. With such encourage-ment the set-dancers usually finished a set in a red-faced welter of perspiration and breathlessness, as they wheeled their partners in one final flurry of intricate footwork that often saw sparks flying as studs and tips clashed with the polished flagstone. This probably gave rise to the phrase often used to describe a great dancer, 'He'd knock lightning off the floor!'

In rural west Clare in the forties, attending a Wren Dance was considered the ultimate in entertainment. From past experiences in running successful Wren Dances, an unwritten code of procedure, a code of ethics, had developed, though 'ethics' may be too strong a word! Much effort was needed to organise the big Wran and even greater effort was required to ensure the success of the subsequent Wren Dance. A suitable venue had to be chosen, the quality and quantity of the musicians who should be invited were discussed at length and, even more important, a date had to be decided that would not clash with another dance. These plans were supposed to be a closely-guarded secret but within days they became the worst-kept secret in the area. The reasons for the initial secrecy were many. One of the main reasons was that it would be much better for all concerned if the attention of the local Garda Sergeant was not drawn to the upcoming dance – the less he knew, the better. One or two over-zealous sergeants took an unwelcome interest in Wren Dances because of the alleged entrance fee and the selling of stout at the dance. Naturally, the organisers vehemently denied such malicious allegations, declaring that their Wren Dance was a private party at which everybody present was an invited guest and that the thought of charging a shilling at the door had never even crossed their lily-white minds. However, it was said that on a few occasions a thwarted sergeant had reaped a rich harvest of unlighted bicycles as the merrymakers made their way home in the early hours of the morning!

The attitude of the local parish priest was also a matter for consideration. There were a few who viewed the Wren Dances as a serious danger to the moral welfare of their flock and who took a dim view of any form of social entertainment. Perhaps they felt that a joyless religion ensured eternal salvation. If a person of such beliefs was parish priest in an area, the local big Wran had to tread very carefully in organising their Wren Dance to avoid any confrontation. It may have been for such reasons that friends of my father from a village about four or five miles away asked him for permission to hold their Wren Dance in our house. An added bonus for such an event was the big car-house beside the house which had a smooth concrete floor, ideal for dancing. And so it was arranged – the music and dancing in the car-house and the teas, especially for the ladies, would be served in the kitchen.

Preparations began a week before the big night. I found it all very exciting as I had never seen a Wren Dance. In fact I had never seen a big dance, apart from the occasional few sets during Christmas. But I soon became an authority on the subject, especially in the school yard! All the hay-making machinery was removed from the car-house and parked in the shelter of the haybarn. Everything was moved out. The walls were given a fresh coat of whitewash and the doors and window frames repainted with the usual red oxide paint. It was only when the car-house was empty that I realised how big it was. A few days before the dance, some men arrived to give it the final touches. The concrete floor was washed and scrubbed with boiling water and some coloured streamers were strung along the walls and across the bare rafters. The place was transformed!

The day before the dance, a *meitheal* or group of women arrived with their menfolk to complete the preparations. They brought with them all kinds of bread and sweet cake with raisins and currants, despite the great scarcity of dried fruit. There were a couple of cooked smoked hams and several cooked geese. The big square table in the parlour was laden down with food, and the beautiful smells made my mouth water with anticipation. Unfortunately, the parlour was made a restricted area for me to which I was denied access. But I still managed to sneak in a few times and pick at some of the raisins on the outside of the cakes!

Meanwhile the men were working hard in the car-house. Several long stools were placed around the walls and when the supply of stools ran out, makeshift seating was made from long planks of timber. Three doors were removed from their hinges in other sheds and used to make a raised platform or stage for the musicians, at the western end of the car-house. At the other end, near the big sliding entrance door, a rough counter was erected from which the patrons would be served the black liquid refreshment. Inside the counter on a raised stand stood a row of red-leaded timber stout barrels , or 'quarter-casks' as they were called, ready for tapping. Stacked high against the wall were several timber crates of lemonade and orange crush, in which I showed a remarkable interest. Several oil lamps were filled with paraffin and hung at intervals around the walls, with wicks trimmed and globes polished and with the usual hairpin balanced on the tops to prevent them cracking. One man brought his Tilley lantern which he hung high among the rafters. This type of lamp was pumped like a primus stove and, when lighted, the small white 'mantel' gave a brilliant white light, much more power-ful than even a double-burner oil lamp. The only drawback was the continuous hissing noise it made. One man was assigned to looking after the lamps for the night. Every detail was taken into account because their reputation as a good Wren group was at stake and serious mistakes or oversights might well be forgiven, but never forgotten!

All the farm chores were finished quickly the evening of the dance. There was a buzz of excitement around the house. Supper was earlier than usual, the kitchen was tidied and both the oil lamp in the kitchen and the table lamp in the parlour were lit. This was also one of the rare times when there was a fire in the grate in the parlour. It seemed to change the whole atmosphere in the room, making it very cosy and warm. My father gave himself an extra careful shave and put on his best clothes. I overheard several of his 'prayers' as he struggled to attach the white starched collar to his shirt, using two studs, one at the back and another at the front. Mother eventually went to his rescue and then helped him with his tie. He looked so much younger when he was dressed up like that! Mother fussed about the house, postponing the changing into her best outfit until the last minute as she found so many little chores to complete first. I didn't escape either! I got an unmerciful washing and scrubbing that temporarily dampened my enthusiasm. I emerged clean as a whistle from the ordeal which I had considered to be totally unnecessary, and was dressed in my Sunday clothes. Dad told me I could stay up late but 'not too late'.

The first to arrive were the women who would look after the teas. They came on their bicycles and trooped into the kitchen, carrying their lamps, and some of them also had their bicycle pumps in their hands. When Dad made a joke about their not trusting the boys from his former parish with the bicycle pumps, one of them quickly retorted, 'It's not that I doubt their honesty, it's just that I'm removing the temptation!' Within an hour, hordes of people arrived in every mode of conveyance. Some had walked, while many had brought their bicycles, often giving a lift to a friend on the crossbar. A few came in their ponies and traps, complete with a candle-lit lantern in case they should meet a patrolling Garda. The ponies were unhitched and tied to the iron pillars of the hay-barn where they had their own 'party' with all that hay beside them. The ladies were dressed in their finery while the men wore their best navy-blue serge suits and white shirts with collars and ties. Many of them looked uncomfortable in the strangling embrace of the over-starched collars. Their discomfort could only get worse as the night wore on, but etiquette, and the watchful eye of their spouse, demanded that the front stud of their collar remain closed! Among the sombrely dressed men, a few extroverts stood out from the rest. Like flashy peacocks, they nonchalantly paraded in view of the girls. Invariably they wore a lighter shade of blue suit or even a light brown one, a bright canary handknitted pullover and highly polished brown shoes. Their hair was plastered down with an over-liberal application of brilliantine that glistened under the soft light of the oil lamps. The new 'rage' at the time, a silvery wristlet watch, was worn well down on the wrist where it was visible to all. These watches were widely advertised at the time by a firm of Dublin jewellers at the special price of a shilling a week for thirty weeks, though how many were fully paid off was open to speculation! Most of the men rolled their overcoats or 'top-coats' into a ball and shoved them under the seats while the ladies left their coats and headscarves draped over chairs and beds in the house.

In a very short time the place was black with people. I thought everybody in Clare must be present! The men wanted to begin dancing to warm themselves. All the musicians had arrived but were clustered around the makeshift bar-counter, getting properly 'lubricated' before taking to the stage. My father produced the gramophone, his beloved Victrolla, which he had brought with him from America with a good supply of Michael Coleman records. I was given the job of helping my neighbour Eileen to change the records, replacing the needles when they got too scratchy and winding the gramophone with the handle at the side, being very careful not to overwind the spring. The lively music filled the car-house and two, sometimes three, sets took the floor at the same time. All the cares, worries, problems and scarcities were forgotten as the happy smiling couples swirled around the concrete floor. Shouts of delight and encouragement rang through the rafters. After a while the musicians took to the stage, the few drinks having worked wonders on their good humour. There were some fiddlers, a few flute players, two with concertinas and one with a battered melodeon. At least ten minutes were spent tuning the instruments, tightening the strings, putting resin on the bows or calling for the concertina player to 'Gimme that high C again, like a good man.' At last they declared themselves in total harmony. Gnarled fingers, hardened and toughened by years of hard work with a shovel or fork, gently caressed the strings of the violin or flashed up and down the keyboard of the melodeon or concertina with a touch as light as a feather. Local musicians were considered a special breed, their gift of music making them welcome in every home. They never received payment for their night's work; their only reward was the joy of playing and their love of the traditional music. They struck up the first tune that set feet a-tapping. The Wren Dance was in full swing!

I watched in admiration as the dancers performed the intricate movements of the different sets and wished I was older, bigger and able to dance! I made sure to visit the drinks area from time to time where somebody always noticed my presence, asked me if I was enjoying the dance and gave me a bottle of lemonade. I kept constantly on the move between the dance and the kitchen where the ladies were serving the teas. I was having a wonderful time as slices of sweet cake, biscuits, pieces of ham and goose were gratefully accepted and devoured until a point was reached very quickly when I didn't want to even look at the food. Going back to the car-house, I was just in time to see Dad and Mother dancing a Caledonian set. I was amazed to discover that they could dance! I realised that I had never even considered the possibility. Dad was an excellent set-dancer. Suddenly I felt very proud of them as they wheeled and 'battered' the floor with the best of them. I was learning more about parents every day!

They never ceased to surprise me!

Occasionally the musicians took a few minutes rest from their endeavours, leaving the stage to 'stretch their legs' and have a well-earned drink or two. During such breaks, we were treated to a song, some step-dancing or even a recitation from somebody on the floor who was pushed forward, however reluctant, by friends. The songs were old, the words known to all, yet the singer always got everybody's full attention with everyone joining in the chorus like one huge family. The spirits of a whole community were lifted by such a night of fun and enjoyment. One elderly man summed it up when he turned to his companion and remarked, 'Tis a night like this that makes it all worthwhile!'

Sometime after midnight, despite my best efforts, my eyes were refusing to stay open any longer. I fought it off for a while but the combination of the food, the lemonade and the excitement finally took its toll. I told Mother that I wanted to go to bed – just for an hour, of course, and then I would get up again. Several of the ladies had left their coats draped across the foot of my bed as they had used the mirror on the dressing table to make last-minute adjustments and repairs to their make-up. My last waking memory was the beautiful scent of face powder and perfume that filled the small room. When I woke again it was late morning. The crowds had left for home as the first rays of the wintry sun peeped over the hills to the east. The Wren Dance would be a topic of conversation around many a turf fire for a week or more. Life returned to normal. The machinery was back in the car-house by late evening. It was as though the Wren Dance had never taken place. No visible signs remained, just indelible memories. The aroma of the powder and perfume lingered in my room for several days.

CHAPTER 12

A Broken Wing

There was a war in Europe! Of that there was no doubt. Many household goods had been scarce in the thirties but now the existence of war was indicated by an even greater degree of scarcity. But it was a boon to the fireside conversationalists. The two mainstays of conversation, the weather and the price of yearlings or calves, lost ground steadily to the new war-induced topics – the discovery of new-found local sources of tea, sugar, flour or cigarettes and, of course, the progress of the war in Europe. Local self-appointed analysts listened carefully to the news on Raidio Éireann and even to the BBC when the wet-battery was fully charged. They then gave to a willing audience their views and profound conclusions, which had to be altered from week to week as predictions failed to come true. They had what appeared to be well-informed fireside discussions, liberally sprinkled with the new jargon of 'offensive movements', 'counter-attacks' and 'pincer attacks' and spoke with great familiarity about the Allied Forces and the Axis, though the latter often suffered in the translation, sometimes being referred to as the 'Axles Forces'. But to us, the children of the period, the war was like a far-off football match that went on, day after day. We wanted the Allies to win the match because we gathered from overheard conversations that they were the 'good guys'. We inwardly felt that each Allied soldier wore the beloved red and green jersey of our own parish beneath his khaki tunic while the German soldier must surely be wearing the hated jersey of the 'townies' from five miles up the road!

The flotsam washed up on the nearby beaches gave silent evidence of the distant war. But as the war progressed, a new alien sound occasionally invaded the quiet countryside. It was the noise of aeroplane engines! Initially, every man, woman and child on hearing the drone of approaching aero engines, rushed into the open to get a good look at the new marvel of the world which defied the laws of gravity and which to many even defied the laws of God. Every tiny speck in the sky was followed with shaded eyes until it disappeared from view. Sometimes the planes were so near that the insignia on the fuselage could be clearly seen, the German swastika, the roundels of the RAF or the White Star of the US Air Force. But within a short time, fear replaced fascination, especially at night time. The roar of low-flying aircraft struck terror into the heart of everybody, the fear of a dropping bomb or of strafing by machine guns.

In those early days of aircraft navigation, many planes lost their way over the darkened land. A number of German bombers, after a bombing raid over England, took the safer round-about route over the west of Ireland to get back to Germany, only to run out of fuel, either through miscalculation or because of bullet-punctured fuel tanks. Many crews baled out of their stricken aircraft and were interned for the remainder of the war—more commonly called the 'duration'! But a number of crews did not have time to bale out and paid the supreme penalty. There were many unsung heroes along the western seaboard who risked their lives to rescue airmen who had crashed into the sea within sight of the shore.

Whenever a plane crash-landed, the news spread like wildfire. Sightseers flocked in every available mode of conveyance to see the remains of what had been, a short time ago, a magnificent flying machine. It was quickly realised that the debris of a crashed plane could be a source of many useful items that would prove invaluable around a farm. There was an endless supply of nuts and bolts, sheets of aluminium from the fuselage, perspex windows, doors and occasionally an unused silk parachute, which was often a boon to some lucky housewife who quickly converted it into dresses, blouses or shirts for her family. The curved aluminium sheets were hammered flat and used to make shed doors, hen-houses or even lean-to sheds. The local Guards moved in to the crash site as quickly as their bicycles would allow, to stop such salvage attempts, and guarded the debris pending the arrival of the Irish army. The crowds scattered, usually as evening milking time approached, and the Guards too went home to their supper. On many occasions the Guards discovered on arriving back at the crash site on the following morning, that the local 'souvenir hunters' had no objection to working at night! This error of judgement was soon rectified.

One warm summer's night, we were all rudely awakened by the thunder of spluttering aircraft engines as a plane passed directly over our house. The whole house seemed to rattle and vibrate with the volume of sound. I cowered beneath the blankets, expecting the plane to crash through the roof. Then the deafening noise faded a little as the plane flew off and, within a matter of a few seconds, seemed to stop abruptly. Picking up the remnants of my courage, I raced barefooted through the kitchen to my parents' room at the far end of the house. They too were wide awake. Somehow it felt safer with Mother and Dad in the room! Mother reassured me that there was no danger and that the plane was gone and wouldn't return. Dad got up and went to the front door. The countryside was silent once more except for the barking of some dogs in the distance – still protesting at the noisy intrusion from the stranger in the sky. It took a long time to get back to sleep! Early the following morning, Dad heard that the plane had crashed into a hillside about three miles away. All the German crew had baled out safely, several miles up the coast and were already on their way to an internment camp in the Curragh for the 'duration'.

Petey and Bridgie lived about a mile from our house, on a small farm of three or four cows. Petey was a small dapper man, very trim and tidy, with his peaked cap perched on the side of his head, almost covering one ear. Bridgie was tall, gaunt and humourless, with a rapier-like tongue that had put many a man in his proper place. Every day, they worked side by side on the farm, sharing the labour. Bridgie preferred the farmwork as good housekeeping was not one of her strong points. They had married rather late in life, much too late to be blessed with a family. While Petey claimed on many occasions, especially after a few pints of stout, that he was 'king of his own castle', everybody knew that Bridgie was the 'high king'! For reasons best known to himself Petey always referred to her as 'the Virgin', though never in her presence! He often began a story with phrases such as, 'Meself and the Virgin were walking home from Mass when …' or 'The Virgin was telling me the other night that …'

The morning after the crash of the German bomber dawned bright and sunny. I gave several unsubtle hints that I would love to see the downed plane, but to no avail. The meadow beside the road had been mown and, given such a beautiful day, the hay should be saved and tied down securely in trams by late afternoon. However, the following day being Sunday,

Dad promised that he would take me on the bar of his bicycle to see the aeroplane. He kept his promise. Giving one's word or making a promise was considered sacred in our house, should never be made lightly, and above all, should never be broken.

By mid-morning we were in the meadow. With the two-pronged hay fork, Dad turned and shook loose the heavier clumps of hay. I valiantly tried to help. The fork was a little too big for me as I tried in vain to match his smooth movements. The prongs of my fork kept sticking in the ground. Allied to that, my hands were being chafed, especially the area between the thumb and forefinger, by the rough handle of the fork. My initial enthusiasm waned rapidly. I found that playing in the meadow or jumping over the bigger clumps of hay was much less demanding and far more enjoyable.

A welcome diversion appeared on the road, a strange contraption approaching slowly over the brow of the hill! As it came closer, I recognised Petey on his donkey and cart. It was immediately obvious that Petey had gone 'shopping' to the crash-site in the very early morning, possibly to avoid both the inevitable crowd of sightseers and the Guards. He stopped to have a few words with my father. He sat in the middle of the donkey cart like a king on his throne, a monarch surveying his realm from a lofty position. His throne was the well-padded, high-backed pilot's seat from the aircraft, now securely tied to the cart with *súgán* ropes. Behind him were four or five concave sheets of aluminium which had once been part of the fuselage.

Highly amused at the incongruous picture presented by Petey and the items he had 'rescued' from the downed aircraft, my father asked him, 'Petey, what in the name of God have you got in the cart?' Taking the evil-smelling pipe from his mouth, Petey slapped a grimy gnarled hand on the padded arm-rest of the pilot's seat and replied with a toothless grin, 'Be Jaysus, Pat, I have a soft "sate" for the Virgin and the makin's of a coop for the hens!'

CHAPTER 13

The Teacher and
The Kaiser

Our house was on the side of a hill with an open front yard beside the main road. Perhaps that was one reason for the constant stream of casual visitors to our door, but I feel that the major reason was that the kettle always seemed to be on the boil and Mother always reached for the teapot the moment a caller arrived. People walking or cycling to the village for their 'messages', as the household shopping was called, were only too willing to rest for a few minutes and have a chat with mother over a cup of tea. All were made welcome, though there were one or two notable exceptions who were quite willing to take advantage of Mother's kindness and generosity in their pursuit of any morsel of gossip. 'Melted rogues,' my father called them, 'dangerous gossip collectors, sitting on their arses all day talking, getting ABC on their shins from the fire – and tea a £1 a pound!'

Dad had a great mistrust of people who 'carried stories' and had a frigid welcome for any caller who was a confirmed gossip. Mother didn't have such strong convictions, but was a good listener who never repeated what she heard. I discovered Dad's low tolerance level for gossip the hard way. On one occasion I overheard some neighbours discussing the rather delicate condition of a local girl and the steps that were being taken to get her married as quickly as possible. Quite frankly, I didn't understand what they were talking about, but it appeared to be a prime item of news. Delighted with my discovery, I rushed home, where Mother and Dad were having a cup of tea in the kitchen, and began to pour forth my great story in a torrent of words, with barely a pause for breath. Before I got to the end of my tale, Dad gave me such a box on the ear with his open hand that I staggered backwards and finished up sitting on the floor. 'Never, never,' he warned me with pointed, wagging finger, 'bring a story into this kitchen or out of it!' I was shocked and dismayed at this total lack of appreciation of my big story. It was a lesson that was never forgotten. From that day forward, I appeared to have lost all interest in gossip!

One regular caller to our house was an unmarried retired teacher, known to all and sundry as Kate the JAM – she had been a Junior Assistant Mistress for many years. She lived alone and, with time heavy on her hands, she spent most of her days walking the three or four miles to and from the village, stopping at several houses along the way for a rest and a chat. The duration of each visit would depend on how busy the host housewife happened to be on that particular day, or would last until Kate sensed that her welcome was wearing thin. An inveterate talker, she spoke in what was known locally as a very 'posh slang', though nobody remembered her having lived outside the borders of the county. One irritating habit which she retained from her years of teaching was to correct pronunciation or grammatical errors in the course of a conversation. In school, she had tried to sow the seeds of elocution, though most of her efforts fell on stony ground. While she loved the semantics of the English language, she detested any form of vulgar expressions. In the classroom one day, she taught her young charges how to identify, and of course spell, the names of a few of the common flora of the area, concentrating on the buttercup and the dandelion. At the end of the class, she held up a piece of a dandelion and asked one boy to identify it. 'A piss-a-bed, Miss,' he told her proudly, to her great horror!

Mother always had a welcome for Kate and gave her the usual cup of tea, as she felt that Kate was a very lonely person, having no close family. One couldn't blame her for walking the roads each day to meet and talk to people because she lived in a very lonely and isolated place – almost a mile from the main road on a narrow winding side-road, with a long muddy boreen, or 'avenue' as it is called in west Clare, which led up to her small neat house with stone-lined flower beds in front. Dad was a little suspicious of her, even though she was more a harmless busybody than a gossip. However, she was nowhere near the top of his 'blacklist'. In his estimation, there were four types of gossip-monger. The worst was the 'malicious gossiper' who should be avoided at all costs. His second type was the 'horse-trader gossiper' who collected and divulged gossip on the basis of 'I'll-tell-you-if-you'll-tell-me'. Next on his list was the 'blabber gossiper' who had a compulsion to blurt out everything to any listener. And finally, the 'squirrel gossiper', who collected and hoarded every nugget of gossip for the sheer enjoyment of possessing it. Kate would fill a minor role in this last category.

Kate the JAM had a passion for hats. But she was very particular about her choice of headgear. Small hats, 'pill-boxes' and turbans she detested, dismissing them out-of-hand because, as she often proclaimed, 'They do nothing for my face!' Well out of earshot and out of range of her sharp tongue, there were many who suggested that there was not yet a hat manufactured that would 'do anything' for her aquiline features! Her great favourite was the broad-brimmed picture hat. She had them in every conceivable shade and design. She was a hat addict! Advertisements in the papers were scrutinised, designs were studied carefully and requests were dispatched for samples to be sent to her on 'fourteen-day approval'. She was a valued customer of several of the leading millinery houses in Dublin who frequently sent her several samples of their current line in picture hats from which she could choose one, returning the others within the specified time. Each hat came separately packed in its own round cardboard hat-box, clearly marked in large red letters, 'DON'T CRUSH'.

Kate's second love was the spread of Christianity in the mission fields of Africa and the Far East. She wrote to every missionary society, answering every appeal for funds. Her charitable disposition assured her of constant reading material, as a fresh supply of booklets, leaflets and letters arrived almost every day in the post.

The man who now delivered the post each day was a character in his own right. Nicknamed The Kaiser, he was a veteran of the First World War. Under the influence of a few pints of stout, he loved to talk about his war exploits in the trenches, leading one to believe that the Great War was a personal two-man battle between himself and the great German emperor, which, of course, he won handsomely! He was a tall, wiry grey-haired man with a clipped moustache and an erect military carriage. To his credit, he could be a very entertaining person, a gifted storyteller, but on the debit side he was a most short-tempered, peevish man who complained continuously about the trials and tribulations of his postal route which, in fairness, covered a myriad of lanes and by-roads. Whenever he was in a bad mood, his wide-ranging vocabulary was not suitable for mixed company! Having heard him in full spate on several occasions, it seemed a good idea at the time to use some of his more colourful phrases in my own conversation. That experiment was a disaster! When Fred the sheepdog playfully jumped up on me and knocked me into a puddle of muddy water, I shouted abuse at him, borrowing some of The Kaiser's language to emphasise my displeasure. It was one of the very rare occasions when Mother lost her temper. Giving me a solid clip on the ear, she warned me against ever again using such 'soldier talk' and threatened that next time she would wash out my tongue with soap because bad curses, just like lies, put a big black mark on one's tongue. Even Fred looked chastened! Furtively, I later checked my tongue in the mirror but the black spot seemed to have worn off!

The Kaiser had developed his own letter-sorting system. The first leg of his route was from the village post-office to our house. After a quick cup of tea, he then sorted the letters in the proper sequence for the next leg of his route, using the big kitchen table as a desk. Kate the JAM was the bane of his life! The letters for her from the various religious orders gave rise to a relatively mild stream of curses, but the arrival of several hat-boxes heralded a cascade of profanities that flowed from his tightly-drawn lips. On such a 'bad' morning, he could be heard approaching the house even before he came into view. With the front carrier of his bicycle piled high with swaying hat-boxes which could not be tied down tightly because of their fragile nature, he repeatedly announced sharply to the silent hedgerows that, 'I should have stayed in the f...ing trenches in France where I was happy instead of pushing a load of f...ing hats around the country for a *Mati Hari* of a woman who orders them just to aggravate me!' After the calming cup of tea, The Kaiser began to sort the letters for the next section, muttering all the time to himself. It was only when a letter for Kate appeared that he seemed to move into a higher gear. Each letter for her evoked the same greeting, without fail. Slamming it on top of the growing pile, he said with deep feeling, 'Christ, Kate the JAM, DON'T CRUSH!' and thus their private war continued day after day!

CHAPTER 14

Love and Marriage

A few miles from our house, two brothers in their fifties lived on a very comfortable farm. Neither of them had ever seriously considered marriage. For many years, they had been very good friends with my father and often came to visit. Both were quiet, honest, hard-working men, simple in their tastes and outlook. Jim was the older of the two and made all the decisions, while Joe was easygoing and very happy with this arrangement. Despite several failed previous efforts, a local matchmaker eventually brought news of 'the possibility of a match with a fine cut of a girl with a bit of money'.

Having assessed the proposal from all angles, Jim saw the positive side of such a marriage and delegated Joe as the future bridegroom. Joe had no objection to Jim masterminding the arrangements and was secretly pleased that Jim regarded him so highly and was so unselfish! The 'writings' were duly signed in a solicitor's office and the marriage ceremony was arranged to take place some two weeks later, on a date suitable to both parties. On the night of the signing of the marriage agreements, the traditional 'picking the gander' party and dance took place in the future bride's home. The event was given this strange title because custom demanded that a goose or, if possible a gander, be killed for the occasion, and the locals discussed the implications of married life with the blushing bride-to-be as they plucked, or 'picked', the goose. (Incidentally, another custom which was strictly adhered to in those days was that the bride could not enter her old home for any reason until thirty days after her marriage, probably with a view to giving her time to recover from any homesickness she might be feeling and to allow her time to settle in her new home. On the thirtieth night after the marriage, another big party and dance was arranged by the bride's family to welcome her back with her new husband for a visit. This night of celebration and dancing was called the 'hauling home'.)

However, it was said that Joe took his upcoming marriage very calmly, didn't foresee any major changes in his set way of life, and assumed that he and Jim would continue more or less as usual, with a few minor adjustments here and there. The main benefit of the marriage, as he saw it, was that he would now be relieved of his duties of cooking and washing, leaving him freer to help Jim with the work on the farm. It would be well worth the inconvenience of having a stranger in the house, to get away from the kitchen!

It was a quiet wedding and after the ceremony the small group had a meal in a restaurant, better known as an 'eating house'. That was the grand total of their honeymoon! As a few of the neighbours were helping to milk the cows and do the other chores around the farm, Jim, Joe and the new bride were in no hurry home and decided to 'make a day of it', arriving home just before dark. After their tea, at which the two brothers displayed their best table manners, they pulled their chairs closer to the fire to have their first quiet chat. Suddenly there was a loud knock on the door and in trooped the first batch of *bacachs*, or strawboys, heavily disguised and with their own musicians, as was the centuries-old tradition. They danced a few sets, the leader of the group asking the bride to be his partner for the first dance. Each of the group silently toasted the bride and groom with a bottle of stout or a *deorum* of whiskey. The leader of the *bacach*s, who was the only one permitted to speak, wished Joe and his bride a happy and fruitful marriage, using an age-old wedding greeting in Irish which was, one could suggest, half-prayer, half-curse. The Irish verse, a verbal tongue-twister, loses much of its impact in the translation:

> May your family have a family
> And their family, have a family.
> And may the person who says
> That your family will not have a family,
> Never have a family of their own.

The first group had left only a few minutes when the next group arrived, following the same procedure. Group after group came and went until it was almost midnight. The popularity of a couple could be judged fairly accurately by the number of *bacach*s who took the trouble to disguise themselves in old clothes stuffed with hay and straw and visit the newly-weds on their wedding night. Joe and his new wife were obviously very well liked and popular. By the time the last group had left, the three of them were tired. It had been a wonderful day that would always be remembered. After a few more minutes' conversation, the new lady of the house declared that she was exhausted and decided that she would retire for the night. She went up the short stairs and disappeared inside the door of the garret which was, in fact, the bedroom occupied by Joe for many years.

Rumour has it that the two brothers pulled their chairs closer to the fire to discuss the events of the day. They tried to recall when was the last occasion they had drunk so much stout. Both agreed that the new wife was a lovely person, good-humoured and pleasant and that they were indeed very

126

lucky. After some time Jim queried, 'Aren't you going to bed at all, Joe?' Having considered the question for a moment, Joe replied, 'Ah sure, we'll give her a few minutes to settle down.' The conversation dragged on for another half-hour. Joe showed no inclination to go to bed, continuing a desultory conversation despite Jim's many pointed glances at the big eight-day clock on the wall.

Eventually Jim's patience ran out! It was time to put a stop to this charade, this dilly-dallying! Turning to Joe with a scowl, he snapped, 'Th' honour of God, Joe, what'll that decent woman think of you at all after you marrying her this very day? Get up them stairs right now, me boy, and no more of your nonsense!' Tightlipped, Joe stood up and started to walk slowly towards the foot of the stairs. With one foot on the first step, he turned rebelliously to Jim and said to him in a voice full of exasperation, 'Listen here to me now, boy, I'm getting right fed-up of you bossing me around and telling me what to do just because you're three years older than me. How come that whenever there's a job to be done around here, 'tis I have to do it?'

As soon as Joe disappeared into the garret, Jim pulled his chair closer to the dying fire to warm his stockinged feet and have one last smoke of his pipe. He thought things over and came to the conclusion that he had made the right decision in getting Joe married. She was a fine sensible girl and he couldn't think of even one reason why all three of them shouldn't be very happy together. He couldn't foresee any dramatic changes being made around the house and looked forward to an improvement in the standard of meals because, to be truthful, Joe's cooking had become very predictable!

Filled with those contented thoughts, so the story goes, Jim set about raking the fire for the night. He placed several sods of turf lengthways around the dying embers of the fire, so that they would smoulder slowly rather than burn rapidly. He quickly shovelled ashes, from the ashpit beside the hearth, on top of the fire. Clouds of fine ash dust billowed around the kitchen, depositing a fine film over everything. Whipping off his cap, he beat at the ash-dust in an effort to send it all up the chimney. He hoped she wouldn't notice the ashes in the morning! He started to undress beside the fire as he had done for many years, throwing his trousers and shirt over the back of a chair where they would be cosy and warm in the morning. Standing there in his vest and 'long-johns', he suddenly thought about the new woman in the house. Slowly picking up his trousers and shirt, he carried them with him to his own bedroom off the kitchen. He began to have the first tinges of misgivings about the new arrangements! She was in the house only a few hours, she hadn't said a word about changes, and already changes were taking place! Maybe he himself should have got married rather than Joe? 'No,' he decided after considering it for a few minutes, 'there's no need to rush into that kind of situation!' He was contented again and didn't mind making a few minor adjustments because of Joe's new wife. Jumping into his cold bed, he pulled the blankets over his head with the comforting thought, 'Ah, wisha, 'tis a bad man that wouldn't warm himself!'

CHAPTER 15

The Harvest of the Strand

The quality of the land in our area was rather poor and demanded great effort to maintain the fertility of the soil. The small size of the farms did not encourage the rotation of patches of gardens for potatoes and root crops. As the same areas were tilled year after year, some form of fertiliser had to be used to counter-balance the mineral deficiency of the ground. The best, and the most common, was farmyard manure, euphemistically called 'top dressing'. However, this was a limited resource which had to be spread evenly over meadows and gardens. The average farm rarely had enough to complete the job in any one year. All along the western seaboard, seaweed was used as a secondary fertiliser, especially in potato gardens. By modern standards it would be considered a very inefficient substitute, but in the thirties and forties it was the only alternative and much sought after.

We were fortunate to be living less than two miles from the sea. Each spring, my father prepared the bog-gardens, ploughing long rows of drills for the sowing of the seed potatoes, which had been sprouting over the winter in a dark shed. On alternative years, he used seaweed in the gardens, saving the 'top-dress' for the meadows. A balance had to be maintained!

Being raised so close to the coast, the sea became part of my world. Growing up, it always filled my western horizon.

It was visible from our house. It was visible from every field. It was always there in the distance. My father, like many others, had learned to recognise the different moods of the sea and could accurately forecast the weather for a particular evening or the following day. The changing colour of the sea to a dark brown-blue indicated approaching rain. The louder roar of the surf in the distance, coupled with the arrival inland of flocks of seagulls, heralded an approaching storm. The farmer working in his fields, especially at hay-making time, always kept a close watch on the sea. An incoming shower was visible while it was still up to twenty miles away, giving at least half an hour's warning. The signs were there to be read by those who could read them.

We lived in that border area where two cultures overlapped – the culture of those who harvested the land and that of those who harvested the sea. Around the fire on a winter's night, stories were told of people and times past. Perhaps half of these stories and yarns were in some way connected with the nearby sea – the lore of the mackerel and herring fleet, the taking of horses or cattle across the one-mile channel to Mutton Island for the summer grazing, or about tragedies at sea. The lore of the sea was interwoven with the lore of the land. I have always loved the sea. It was part of the familiar home scene to me. But I was also aware of the different moods of the ocean, from the lapping of wavelets on the summer beach to the angry winter roar of mountainous waves as they attacked the restraining cliffs and sand dunes. I have learned to have the utmost respect for the power, the might and the majesty of the sea. Old fishermen will say that the sea is unforgiving. They believe that a person will rarely be allowed by the sea to make a second serious mistake in a curragh, as the first one usually finishes in tragedy.

Drawing seaweed from the strand for the gardens was

always a joy to me. The high turf-creel was put on top of the horse cart and I was allowed to stand in the car beside my father, looking over the top of the creel at the changing countryside as Grey Fann jogged along towards the coast. By merely looking at the changing house styles, one could see the subtle shift from the 'farm culture' to the 'fishing culture'. The first noticeable feature was the different style of thatching. Around our own home, most of the houses were sew-thatched, with either wheat or barley straw, with an average lifespan of ten to fifteen years. Near the sea, most of the houses were thatched with a blanket of rushes, held in places with a network of *súgán* or cord, with a lifespan of two or three years. The houses appeared to be smaller, though very picturesque because of the brilliant whitewash and the green thatch.

The twelfth-century church ruin, Cill Mhuire, seemed to mark the border between the two zones. The old church from which our parish took its name was once the centre of a densely populated village, Tromera, which stretched from the church to the sea. For some reason, probably poverty, the village slowly declined. The Great Famine was the final blow. The village virtually disappeared. A new parish church was built two miles inland in another village. Of the old church, all that remained were the stone walls and the surrounding cemetery. A few well-scattered houses were the only survivors of the former clustered village settlement. But the ivy-covered heaps of stones, the dark green grassy mounds, the briars growing through cracked flagstones all give silent testimony to what was once a vibrant community. As we jogged along in the horse and cart, my father showed me the faint outlines of scores of house foundations and the wide grassy square, still called the Fair Green, which was used as a famine graveyard during the final death throes of the forgotten village of Tromera.

A little beyond the old church ruins, the fresh smell of the sea became more pronounced. The sound of the surf could be heard as we climbed the last low hill. The houses became more and more plentiful and the columns of turf smoke pointed softly heavenwards from each chimney. The people obviously took great pride in their homes. All were neatly painted, mostly white but with the occasional pink or blue. Windows and doors were freshly painted too and the front yards were covered with flagstones or fine gravel. Well-tended flower beds were lined with rows of whitewashed round stones from the strand. Many houses had lobster pots, made with sally rods, stacked at one gable of the house while several had fishing nets drying on the grass. Nearer the shore, almost every house had an upturned curragh resting on timber stands in the lee of the house, often covered with wet sacking to protect the tarred canvas outer skins from cracking under the heat of the sun.

The sound of the iron wheel-bands on the gravelled road brought people to their doors to shout a greeting to us as we passed by. They were a friendly hardworking people. Dad knew them all and paused now and then for a brief word. He always stayed a little longer with one old gentleman, Jim Gallagher, who spoke only in Irish to me, though he also spoke fluent English. He was the last of the native Irish speakers in the area. Everybody else used English, though their English was punctuated with Irish words, with a few curses in Irish thrown in for good measure when the occasion demanded. They were one generation removed from the language of their forebears. The attitude of the educational system to the native language over the previous several decades had encouraged the use of English as being progressive while condemning the use of Irish as a sign of being backward and uneducated. It was only in the twenties and thirties that attempts were undertaken to revive the language, but it was already too late.

We soon reached the coast and turned left on Ardavohar, the road that ran by the edge of the cliff, until we reached Ceann a Vohar, the little road that wended its way down to the beach below. Though English was now the vernacular, the Irish placenames persisted. Every island, every rock, every reef was known by its ancient Irish name – Carraig a Dabh, Carraig Nuala, Carraig na Rón, Na Gandal. We had reached the strand! The rattle of the wheels on gravel became silent as Grey Fann trotted along the hard-packed sand. Great brown mounds of seaweed had been deposited by the retreating tide at several places along the strand. Four or five other people were already there with their horses and carts, on the same errand as ourselves. Local fishermen were cutting off the thick brown stalks of the seaweed, which they would later dry and sell by the ton for a few pounds. It was hard cold work for a meagre return.

My father began filling the creel with the long slippery seaweed. There was a great deal of good-humoured banter between the men as they worked. The strand people were always a happy bunch. The dangers encountered when fishing in their frail curraghs gave them a philosophy which was best summed up by one fisherman, 'Enjoy today and God is good for tomorrow.' I listened in wide-eyed fascination as the fishermen chatted among themselves about where the mackerel and herring were running, about the making of lobster pots or about upcoming weather conditions. But the main topic of conversation was the amount of wreckage, or 'wrack', that was being washed ashore and what each one had found the previous week. The flotsam of war washed up along the strand helped them to survive and to provide for their families. The sinking of merchant ships by the wolf-packs of German U-boats provided a rich harvest of 'wrack'. The reward paid by Dunlops of Cork for finding a bale of rubber on the beach, for instance, varied from five to ten pounds plus a very precious bicycle tyre. Bales of cotton were confiscated by the local police, but the salt water had ruined the cotton which meant there was no monetary reward. Drums of petrol and paraffin oil were the prime target of the confiscating arms of the law. Though there was no official reward for the fishermen who found them on the beach, some of the locals discovered a method of draining off a few gallons from each drum, re-sealing it again before the Guards arrived. Drums of tallow were quickly converted to the manufacture of candles, using an old bicycle pump as a mould and a waxed hemp cord as a wick. Because of the long immersion in salt water, these homemade candles spluttered a lot, but they were a welcome source of light in many homes. Timber was found in abundance, much of which was sold to farmers for a few shillings. They used it to build sheds, gates or even houses. On many occasions, cases of whiskey and rum floated ashore, leading to several impromptu parties to which the Guards would never be invited.

One of the men gave me a fistful of dried sea grass which I chewed as I listened. They told me about huge long sea monsters who swam close to the shore and had a particular weakness for small boys! This, I was solemnly told, was the reason why small boys should only go bathing in summertime in the rock-pools along the beach and not out there among the waves where the monsters lurked. I agreed with those knowing men in their high-necked sweaters, their 'blue ganzies', that the rock-pools would be my choice in the future. I played along the sandy beach for a while, examining the many shells that dotted the area. With a piece of a stick, I drew lines, squares and circles in the sand and even printed my name in big letters near the edge of the water, all the time keeping a sharp look-out for any of those monsters who might suddenly decide to come ashore. All too soon, my father called me and we began our long walk home. The creel was piled high with seaweed and long wet ribbons trailed to the ground like a bridal train as Grey Fann pulled her load up Ceann a Vohar and back on the dusty gravelled main road.

Further along the cliff road, a few fishermen were working beside a long stone-lined pit from which pungent smoke was pouring into the still spring air. It was a most unusual sharp smell. We stopped to exchange a few words with the men. One of them was my Irish-speaking friend, Jim. I had often heard about the burning of kelp, but this was the first time I had seen the operation. A large number of local families had deserted their island homes around the turn of the century and built houses on the mainland. The reason for this migration was the kelp industry, then at its peak. The end product of the burning of the dried seaweed, kelp, was much sought after by a factory in Glasgow where further processes extracted the iodine content. But by 1917 the market for kelp had collapsed with the discovery in Chile of cheaply produced iodine-bearing minerals. But now, because of the war, shipments from Chile were suspended and kelp-burning was resumed for a brief few years before eventually fading into history.

It involved very hard work for a meagre reward. The heavy wet seaweed was carried or dragged to the fields at the rear of the sandhills to be dried until it was crisp. The more fortunate had ponies and carts, but many carried the dripping seaweed in baskets on their backs. It was spread on the grass or laid across wire fences until dry. Small groups of families, working in co-operation, had their own kelp pit – a long, sloping, flag-lined pit, deeper at one end. The dried seaweed was carried to the pit area and built into tall cocks, ready for the next stage.

The fire in the pit was started with an armful of hay. The dry seaweed was added little by little. It was important that the weather was favourable, with the wind blowing across the pit rather than along its length, as the cross-wind ensured an even temperature in all areas of the pit. The men knew by the colour of the flame when the correct temperature was reached. The fire smouldered with an intense heat. Great expertise was needed to keep it burning evenly because a huge flaming fire would reduce all their work and effort to ashes within minutes. They used long-handled forks called 'crooks', with the prongs bent inwards, to tend the fire, as the heat would not permit them to approach too closely. The burnings went on for several days at a time. Each night the fire was allowed to die down and the excess weed was 'crooked' from the liquid that had been extracted from the smouldering seaweed and which now formed a hot pool at the deep end of the pit. By the following morning, the liquid had solidified into a hard, grey, opaque slab. Sledges and crowbars were used to break the slab into manageable pieces, which were then stacked near the pit. Everything was again ready for another day's burning!

During the kelp-burning season, an agent for the Glasgow factory arrived at the local railway station on a particular day each week. His job was to weigh the kelp-slabs of each fisherman and grade their standard of quality, using a chemical solution to establish the iodine content. He also took into account any visible impurities such as stone, sand or pieces of weed embedded in the slabs. On the appointed day the fishermen arrived at the station with their slabs, using any available means of transport – horse carts, ponies and donkeys, some using their own animal, some borrowing a horse for the day, while a few had to hire somebody for a nominal fee. But it was an important day, the day they got paid for their hard work!

However, there was a sting in the tail! That hard-earned money was not yet theirs to take home to their families. When stating that the men who harvested the strand had to work hard for whatever they earned, it should be taken into account that a hundred tons of wet seaweed weighed only thirty tons when dried and produced just one ton of kelp-slab. The price they received for the kelp varied from five to ten pounds per ton depending on the grade, which more often than not was decided on the whim of the agent at the station rather than by chemical analysis. With very rare exceptions, the fishermen owned no land, just their house and a small 'strip' of garden for which they paid an annual rent. Immediately the agent paid them for the kelp-slab, they had to meet their rent commitments even before they left the railway station – being poor and landless had its price tag! One-third of their income from selling the kelp was handed over to the local landlord who owned the shore rights of the strand from which the seaweed was initially collected. A fee of ten shillings per month was charged by the owners or tenant-farmers of the fields and fences on which each fisherman dried the seaweed. All arrears had to be paid promptly, otherwise they would have no place to dry the seaweed for the next burning. It was a vicious treadmill that demanded a constant production of kelp to eke out a mere existence!

Slowly we wended our way homewards, Grey Fann setting her own pace with Dad walking beside her, the reins held loosely in his hand. Sometimes I walked beside him, plying him with questions about the strand or about being at sea in a big ship, as he had been a few times going to and from

America. I tried to visualise a big liner with several decks and cabins, but found it difficult, having never seen any boat bigger than a curragh. Sometimes I walked behind the cart, watching the trailing ribbons of seaweed draw wriggly lines on the dusty road. I kept thinking about the strand and what a lovely happy place it was, the bright sand, the rolling surf, the wheeling seagulls and the jolly fishermen who were all so friendly to me. It presented a very romantic picture, but a six-year-old boy could neither see nor comprehend the hardship and poverty that existed beneath the apparently happy and tranquil surface.

We soon reached home. I was back again in my familiar world. Apart from the distant hum of the surf, the culture and lifestyle of the strand seemed very far away once more. Dad took the load of seaweed to the garden where he would spread it evenly along the furrows between the drills later on that evening. I ran to the kitchen to tell Mother all about my trip to the strand. The smell of cooking made me realise that I was ravenous with the hunger. The sea air gives one an amazing appetite!

CHAPTER 16

A Shepherd to a
Mixed Flock

The Great Famine of 1847 and the much less publicised famine of the 1870s left an indelible mark on the landscape of hundreds of parishes throughout Ireland, including our own. The population of the parish was decimated over a period of about thirty years, from almost twelve thousand to a little over three thousand. But the famines also left an invisible mark on the people of our area, a psychological fear which continued for almost a century of the *fíor gorta*, the 'true hunger' or famine. It gave rise to a survival mentality and a survival economy. This subconscious fear was prolonged by other outside factors which hindered enterprise and development – the First World War, the struggle for independence, the Civil War, the Economic War and finally the outbreak of the Second World War. It was a long turbulent period. The small farmers of west Clare struggled to produce enough food to survive through the long winter and spring months. Life followed a set pattern, year after year. Enterprise or innovation would be courting disaster, and the fear of failure ensured the continuation of the survival economy even into the late 1950s. Some far-seeing person was needed in each area to take the initiative and break the mould. Such a man was our parish priest, Father O'. From the time of his appointment in the mid-1930s until his death in the late 1940s, he strove tirelessly to change old patterns and improve the lot of his flock.

In the area of farming he was a visionary, filled with irrepressible enthusiasm. In retrospect, he was a man before his time, about thirty years too early! Had he not been a churchman, he would have been a wonderful Minister of Agriculture. He advocated the establishment of farming co-operatives long before the word came into common usage. Another of his suggestions was that the cross-breeding of different cattle types should be used to specialise in either better beef production or in increased milk production. Most of his ideas are now accepted practice in modern Ireland, though in the thirties and forties, his advice was secretly scoffed at and ignored. The fear of change created a mighty barrier of resistance to change. Barely ten years after his death, the first cracks appeared in that barrier and the farming community tentatively entered the twentieth century.

While Father O' was not very tall, he was a striking figure in his square Roman biretta and long black leather overcoat. He was a man of many contrasts. He had a quick smile and an equally quick temper. He was kind and gentle, yet could be very fussy, with little patience for bureaucracy or incompetence. A great organiser, he built one of the first parish halls in the county, where plays, concerts and dances helped to raise funds for the parish. At such social occasions, he always got the patrons in good humour with his off-key rendition of the only song he knew, 'Coming through the Rye'. His mode of transportation was a battered Morris 8, its spare wheel strapped on to the back and with very dubious brakes. From a garage-owner friend in the town of Ennistymon, fifteen miles away, a gallon of petrol arrived at the local railway station in a jerrycan each Friday during the war years. Friendship of that high calibre was unique in those years of great scarcity. With good management, that gallon of petrol was sufficient for a week.

Father O's generosity and cheerful disposition ensured a steady stream of callers to his door. He was the Oracle to whom everybody came with their troubles, many of which were very real in those hard times. A few called merely for reassurance rather than for any practical solutions. Many of his visitors were sad, many were interesting and quite a few were amusing. Every Friday, without fail, Cycling Mary called to see him for a chat. She lived a few miles away and walked up the hill past our house each Friday, pushing her bicycle, on her way to the village to collect her aged father's pension. She often called to see my mother, and had a cup of tea before proceeding to Father O's house. She was an honest, simple person who was obsessed with the notion that all her neighbours were talking about her. She bought herself a new bicycle, a 'high nelly', just to show the neighbours that she could afford it and that she 'was as good as the best of them'. For years, that bicycle was her constant companion everywhere she went. She walked beside it because, in all those years, she had never learned to ride it!

The travelling people had a special place in Father O's heart. The different traveller families of those years were well known to every household and were often on a first-name basis. The travelling tinsmith was most welcome at every door as he was the sole source of supply for galvanised buckets, tin cups, billy-cans and pots. Not alone did he make the new utensils, he also provided an after-sales service. He carried with him an array of pot-menders and solder and repaired any leaks that might have developed since his previous visit. Father O' had a special bond with the travelling families. He became their unofficial chaplain, performing countless marriage ceremonies, baptising their children, settling disputes and, above all, being a friend in times of trouble.

One travelling tinsmith who called regularly to see him was Tin-pot Paddy. A well-dressed, smooth, suave talker, Tin-pot travelled the countryside plying his trade, and accompanied by his wife Kitty. He was forever singing Kitty's praises – what a wonderful wife she was and always referring to her as 'me darling Kitty'. Unfortunately, poor Kitty died but, within a matter of months, Tin-pot was married again to another travelling woman, a big burly red-haired fortune-teller nicknamed The Wheels of the World. She quickly asserted her authority and Tin-pot deeply regretted his impetuous second marriage. He found little comfort in telling his tale of woe to Father O' who reminded him that 'If you light your lamp, you have to pay for the oil!' He did not even escape the satirical humour of one of his fellow travellers who wrote a song about 'Tin-pot's' second marriage with the following opening verse:

> Me darling Kitty,
> Wasn't long dead,
> When The Wheels of the World
> Rolled in to her bed.

The improvement of the farming methods of his parishioners was one of Father O's main activities. In this he tried to lead by example. A few fields at the back of his house were used to feed three or four pedigree cows of different breeds which were much superior to the common local breed of Shorthorn. His garden produced all types of vegetables and fruit and his new glasshouse was his pride and joy. While Father O' provided the innovative and creative ideas, Jamesey was his indispensible right-hand man. Jamesey was a

142

character in his own right. With his turned-down pipe and his soft felt hat, he was a man of great wit, a natural homespun comedian. A most happy, cheerful person, his big blue eyes twinkled with 'devilment'. He had that rare quality, a God-given gift, of making people laugh and feel better by merely talking to them for a few minutes. He was responsible for the gardens and the livestock as well as the repair and upkeep of the parish schools and churches. He was the perfect counter-balance for Father O', encouraging him when some scheme failed to work and curbing the good priest's enthusiasm when it bordered on the unreasonable.

One such occasion arose when Father O' decided to show the local farmers the benefits of crossbreeding cattle to increase milk production. Somewhere in County Tipperary he bought a pedigree Whitehead heifer, designated to be the future matriarch of a highly productive herd. The heifer was the first of that particular breed in our area and Father O' took great pride in displaying his new acquisition to the locals and expounding his theories. In due course, the heifer's first calf arrived and Father O's joy knew no bounds. But Jamesey's troubles were only beginning! When he tried to milk her, all hell broke loose! The bucket, the stool and poor Jamesey were sent flying with a barrage of well-aimed kicks from the indignant cow who resented any intrusion of her privacy. It was unfortunate that she was, in fact, that rarity in the bovine world, a cow that refused point-blank to be milked. Jamesey tried coaxing her, calming her, rubbing her, tying her legs together and cajoling her, all to no avail. His 'prayers' flowed in a steady stream through the cowhouse door. Father O' anxiously wrung his hands and encouraged Jamesey to persevere! The sweat rolled in rivulets off Jamesey in his efforts. This continued for a week until, with both Jamesey and the cow in a state of exhaustion, Father O' finally conceded defeat and decided that the cow would be sold immediately. The morning after Father O's welcome decision, Jamesey and the cow set off to walk the five miles to the fair in the local town.

Before leaving for the fair, Jamesey agreed with Father O' on a minimum selling price. Knowing Jamesey's deep dislike for the obstinate cow, the priest gently reminded him to inform any prospective buyer of the cow's unusual problem. Jamesey walked to the fair, praying that he would sell her quickly, because in truth he was utterly exhausted from his efforts to milk her. Within a half-hour of arriving at the fair, the cow was sold for a very good price and Jamesey had a few pints to celebrate the departure of the unlamented animal. He returned home in high spirits. Father O' met him near the front of the house and was amazed and delighted that the cow had been sold for such a good price. 'Had you any trouble in selling her?' he queried. 'Not a bit in God's earth,' Jamesey replied. 'A big farmer from County Limerick bought her in less than two minutes.' Jamesey started to walk towards the kitchen to get something to eat. Looking at the better-than-expected amount of money in his hand, Father O' called after him, 'Are you sure, Jamesey, that you told the man the full story about the cow?' Jamesey stopped and turned towards Father O', 'Did I tell him the whole story, you're asking me? Holy God, Father, I told him he'd be tired from milking her!'

CHAPTER 17

The Parish Mission

Father O' was a firm believer in a parish retreat, better known as a Mission. He often referred to the Mission as a badly-needed 'spiritual spring cleaning'. Every two or three years he arranged for one for the parish. The announcement of the opening of such a Mission struck secret terror into the hearts of many. It was a two-week period of deep religious fervour. Fiery retreat priests, the Missioners, thumped the pulpit, loudly preaching fire and damnation on all evildoers unless they immediately repented. The 'demon drink' took a severe battering as Missioners and wives joined forces to divert thirsty husbands back to the 'straight and narrow path to salvation'. The Friday night of the Mission week was for many the climax of the whole week when the pledge against drink was undertaken by the whole congregation, some gladly, some sadly and some with misgivings. Taking the pledge was a serious matter, not to be done lightly. But old habits are hard to break! On one particular pledge night, two hardened old drinking cronies were walking quickly towards the church gate with very little time to spare. One turned to the other and asked, 'Come here a minute, boy, will we have one last pint before we go inside and take the pledge?' His friend replied, 'Not at all, boy, we haven't time now. We'll wait until we come out!'

One regular visitor to our house, especially during the long winter nights, was Tadhg Neddy who lived about a mile away, between our house and the village. He was an honest hard-working man with a great sense of humour and an endless supply of funny stories. But he had a weakness for a good pint of stout. Fairdays, Sundays and holy days were days on which he over-imbibed, often weaving his way homewards in the late afternoon to a burnt dinner and a not-too-gracious welcome from his long-suffering wife. She had been trying for years to get him 'on the dry' but all efforts had been dismal failures. Every New Year's Day and Ash Wednesday he willingly made an attempt to give up the drink, but after a few days his enthusiasm had waned as he sorely missed the camaraderie of his drinking companions and the taste of a good pint. Intentions were good but the spirit was weak! Tadhg Neddy was a religious man in his own fashion with a great respect for priests. Like many of his generation, he feared their 'powers', being firmly convinced that they had the ability to perform certain miracles should the occasion demand it.

The Mission had just begun in the parish with the Missioners staying in Father O's house, a few hundred yards from Tadhg Neddy's farmhouse. One Missioner in particular was considered a great preacher, as his loud angry words reverberated around the high walls of the church, striking fear into the hearts of sinners and would-be sinners alike. On the Thursday of Mission week, he met Tadhg Neddy's wife as he strolled along the road, reading his breviary. During the course of their very friendly conversation, she found herself telling him about Tadhg's drinking problem and of her many fruitless attempts to convert him to temperance. 'Don't worry, my good woman,' he assured her. 'I'll put the fear of God into him and he'll never drink again.' She was delighted that she had taken such a drastic step. The Missioner went into the potato garden beside the house where Tadhg Neddy was working and accosted him about his evil ways. 'Kneel down right there where you are,' he roared at the trembling Tadhg, 'and repeat the words of the pledge after me.' Tadhg Neddy repeated the words of the pledge, renouncing drink forever. 'And remember one thing, my good man,' the Missioner thundered at him, 'remember I am warning you that if you break that pledge, even have one drink, you have my word for it that you will lose your sight and that you will be blind forever.'

Poor Tadhg Neddy took the Missioner's words seriously and was very scared. He fought off every temptation to have a pint, and there were many. A week after the Mission, most of his drinking companions had 'broken out' and were back on the drink again. But Tadhg kept his dark secret to himself! There were moments when he would gladly have 'given his right hand for one pint'. Passing his favourite pub with the smell of stout wafting out through the open door was agonising, a mighty conflict between the temptation and the priest's dire warning! It became so bad one night that he walked in to the pub, ordered a pint and sat looking at it for almost ten minutes before passing it over to a grateful friend and walking out the door, a sad, confused and very thirsty man! He missed drinking his pint and chatting with his friends and it was proving to be a very heavy burden.

Two days later, he went back to the pub and again ordered a pint. He sat on the high stool, looking at the drink and admiring it for several minutes. His mind was in turmoil! It was decision time! He lifted the froth-topped pint from the counter and walked very slowly to the open door. Raising his pint in a salute, he looked lovingly up at the clear blue sky and the brilliant sunshine and solemnly said with a sigh of resignation as he lowered the glass to his thirsty lips, 'Oh well, goodbye daylight!'

CHAPTER 18

A Man and His Horse

Probably the most essential member of our farm animal family was the big Irish draught horse, Grey Fanny, or Grey Fann as we always called her. She was born on the farm and, even as a foal, was gentle and affectionate and was always treated as a pet. The dark brown silky coat became flecked with grey when she was a yearling and had become white-grey by the time she was fully grown at three years. There was a great bond between my father and Grey Fann, a mutual trust. His love of animals manifested itself most strongly in the caring attention he gave Grey Fann. She was groomed and well-fed and, as my mother often said, he took better care of Grey Fann than he took of himself. In return she was a willing worker who gave of her best at all times. She worked to his instructions or commands, and I can say, without fear of contradiction, that he never used a whip or a stick in their many years together. He detested cruelty to any animal and instantly disliked and mistrusted anyone he saw beating an animal, especially a horse.

Trying to catch a horse in a big open field can be both frustrating and exhausting, especially if the horse prefers not to be caught. My father had a joke which I often heard him tell about the farmer who sent a workman to catch a rather wild horse. The man tried every trick he knew to catch the animal, chasing him into every corner of the field, but still the horse escaped. The horse was enjoying the game but the poor man was exhausted. He lay down in the middle of the field to get his breath back. Eventually the curiosity of the horse was aroused and he approached the prone man slowly to examine him more closely. The man looked up and said to the horse, 'All jokes aside, the boss is looking for you!'

However, my father never had such problems. All he had to do was open the gate, whistle loudly and Grey Fann would come at a gallop. He would then walk up the road to the shed with Grey Fann beside him, playfully nudging his shoulder with her muzzle.

On one particular dark, overcast evening, he went to the gate and gave his usual whistle. Stretching westward from the road were two fields connected by a muddy gap where an old, broken, rusty gate still hung from the stone pier. The gate had not been closed for years and its base was deeply embedded in the mud while the briars had grown over the top bar. However, that evening, unknown to Dad, the pig had escaped from her paddock and strayed into the horse's field. Somehow or other the pig pushed the gate almost closed, probably by scratching herself against it.

When Dad whistled, Grey Fann was grazing in the second field and immediately started galloping for home. At the last moment, my father saw the partially closed gate and shouted, but it was too late! The sharp rusty corner of the top bar of the gate sliced through Grey Fann's flank, partially disembowelling her. Fortunately, she stood there in shock, not moving. Dad ran the length of the field to her as she stood there with blood pouring from the gaping twelve-inch wound in her side. I had run after him, wondering what was happening. He flung the rusty gate aside and gazed at Grey Fann as she stood with trembling legs in the muddy gap. It was the first time in my life I saw my father cry. I had never realised that fathers could cry. Feeling shattered at my discovery, I too cried. But he was talking to Grey Fann, soothing her and reassuring her. 'Easy, girl! Easy, girl!' he kept telling her. 'We'll have to get you home.'

He quickly removed his jacket and threw it to me. Whipping off his shirt, he stood bare-chested in the biting, cold, winter wind and placed the wadded shirt over the gaping wound. She whinneyed softly as though she was in great pain. He kept talking gently to her. He asked her to move forward. She took one tentative step and stopped. He walked sideways with her, holding the makeshift bandage in place with his body. She took another step and rested. It was painfully slow progress. Her head was held very low and her legs were shaking and folding under her. She wanted to lie down but he would not let her, keeping her moving, one step at a time. It was almost two hundred yards to the shed and I felt that she would never make it. But he kept encouraging her, 'One more step, girl. One more step.' I could see the big tears roll down his face as she stretched her head over her shoulder and nuzzled his side.

He told me to run as fast as I could and ask Michael, our neighbour, to cycle to the post office in the village and telephone a friend of his in Kilrush, a veterinary surgeon. My mission accomplished, I told Mother what had happened. She too was shocked, but she remained calm and said that plenty of hot water might be needed. I could hear her praying softly as she hung the kettles over the fire. I ran back to Dad and Grey Fann. They had made some progress, but it was painfully slow. A few neighbours arrived and helped Dad over the final fifty yards. Two of them got the car-house ready, piling plenty of hay on the floor. They got Grey Fann into the car-house and she needed little encouragement from Dad to lie down on the pile of hay, thus taking a lot of strain and pressure off the wound. She lay there, fully stretched out, the whites of her eyes showing her fear and her pain. Putting some disinfectant in the warm bucket of water that Mother had carried from the kitchen, Dad bathed the wound until the vet finally arrived. The neighbours had been shaking their heads, saying she was finished and should be put down to take her out of her misery. Dad angrily refused to accept their suggestions and said he would 'see it out to the bitter end' with her.

I was sent to the kitchen to keep Mother company. I kept asking her if Grey Fann would die. She reassured me that Grey Fann would be all right, if it were God's will. Not being as philosophical as Mother, I could not see why God had to choose Grey Fann when there were so many other horses in the world. I silently asked him, there and then, to leave us Grey Fann because we all loved her and to get Himself another horse from somewhere else. Dad and the vet worked for several hours in the car-house before the vet finally closed the wound with a multitude of stitches and put a large dressing over it. I heard him tell Dad that her chances were slim, but that she might survive if no complications set in. After a cup of tea, he left for home.

Grey Fann lay on the bed of hay, trembling with fever. Dad covered her totally, except for her head, with blankets and hay. He gave her sips of water from a bottle as she couldn't lift her head to drink from a bucket. He kept talking to her and gently rubbing the side of her head. He stayed up all night with her, drinking cups of tea, under the dim light of a candle and a small lantern. His vigil continued the next day and again the following night. Our neighbour, Michael, milked the cows and helped Mother with the other chores. If my father left the car-house for a few moments, Grey Fann whinneyed until he returned. On the morning of the third day, she was able to lift her head and looked a little brighter. That night, Dad slept in close to her and when he woke in the morning, she was trying to stand up. Using ropes thrown over the rafters, he and Michael helped her to stand. It took a little time, but I can still recall the delight and joy on Dad's face. She lay down again after a short time, but the worst was over. She was going to get better. The next time she wanted to stand up, she did it on her own. It was good to have Dad back home at night again. After a week, Grey Fann was allowed to graze in the field for some hours, but it was a few months before she was fit to do even light work again. She carried the long black scar on her side for the rest of her life. The bond of trust between Dad and Grey Fann appeared to be even greater than before!

Twenty years after these events took place, time had taken its toll. Teddy, the little dog, was very old and stiff in his joints and was blind in one eye. Grey Fann was now in well-earned retirement and had become slow-moving and ponderous, but my father still looked after them, making sure they were well fed and had warm shelter at night. Fred, the sheepdog, had been killed several years before by a passing car as he crossed the road. Neither of my parents was enjoying the best of health, probably paying the price for a lifetime of hard work. In the mid-1960s, my mother died after a short illness. After her death, my father appeared to lose interest in life, though he continued to work the farm despite his doctor's orders. He seemed lost without Mother. He died suddenly six months later. They were together again!

I continued to give Teddy his food, but he just sniffed at it and turned away. I now lived a very short distance up the road from the old house, with my own family. It was sad to close the old home after the funeral. Its familiar sounds were now silenced forever. I had become quite worried at Teddy not eating. Three days later, I couldn't find him. My cousin Gerry, now the local vet, helped me search for him. We eventually found him lying dead in the vacant bed in my father's room. He had followed Dad to the end!

For the first few days after my father's passing, Grey Fann grazed peacefully in her field. I continued to take extra care of her, giving her plenty of hay and her daily ration of oats. After about a week, I noticed that she seemed to be spending a great deal of time standing at the gate looking up the road towards the house, with her head erect and her ears pointed forward. Just to be sure, I asked Gerry to examine her. He told me that, taking her age into consideration, she was in perfect physical condition. The watching from the gate continued. Then the loud whinneying began. It continued at intervals, both day and night. She began to gallop around the fields, head erect, eyes searching every nook and cranny. Everybody was convinced that she was searching for my father. What was even more amazing to all who knew her was the fact that she now clambered over high walls and jumped lower ones, something that was totally out of character for her. The whinneying and the searching continued for almost a week. I tried everything I could think of to calm her down, rubbing her white coat, talking to her – all to no avail. After a few minutes, she would wheel away from me and continue her fruitless search. I even put her in the shed for a while, but she pushed down the door. By the end of the week, I was becoming desperate. I discussed the problem at length with Gerry, who finally turned to me and said, 'Let's try something non-medical.' He went to the old house and got one of my father's battered old hats. Coming back to the gate, he held it out to Grey Fann. She sniffed at it a few times and grabbed it between her teeth as I had seen her do so often, many years before. She turned and galloped back to her field. The whinneying and galloping stopped. She began to graze peacefully. We watched her for a long time. 'That's one very lonely horse,' Gerry remarked. 'She's got feeling!'

We left her in her field, happy in the knowledge that her distress had disappeared and that she seemed to have returned to normal. Early the following morning I went down the road to see her. I found her lying dead in a corner of the field, the old hat beside her outstretched head. The last link lay broken on the ground! It marked the end of an era.

Other books from The O'Brien Press

Pictorial Ireland
Yearbook and Appointments Diary
Superb full colour photographs of Ireland's wonderful
landscapes, towns, people. Each year a new diary, available
every summer in advance. *Wiro bound £6.95.*

Irish Life and Traditions
Ed. Sharon Gmelch
Visions of contemporary Ireland from some of its most
well-known commentators — Maeve Binchy, Nell McCaf-
ferty, Seán Mac Réamoinn, Seán MacBride. Deals with nature, cities, prehistory, growing up in Ireland (from the
1890s in Clare to the 1960s in Derry), sports, fairs, festivals,
words spoken and sung. 256 pages, 200 photos.
£6.95 paperback.

Old Days Old Ways
Olive Sharkey
Entertaining and informative illustrated folk history, re-
counting the old way of life in the home and on the land.
Full of charm. *£5.95 paperback.*

Kerry
Des Lavelle and Richard Haughton
The landscape, legends, history and people of a beautiful
county. Stunning full colour photographs. *£5.95 paperback.*

Sligo
Land of Yeats' Desire
John Cowell
An evocative account of the history, literature, folklore and
landscapes, with eight guided tours of the city and county,
from one who spent his childhood days in the Yeats
country in the early years of this century. Illustrated. *£14.95
hardback.*

A Valley of Kings
THE BOYNE
Henry Boylan
An inspired guide to the myths, magic and literature of this beautiful valley with its mysterious 5000-year-old monuments at Newgrange. Illustrated. *£7.95 paperback.*

Traditional Irish Recipes
George L. Thomson
Handwritten in beautiful calligraphy, a collection of favourite recipes from the Irish tradition. *£3.95 paperback.*

Consumer Choice Guide to Restaurants in Ireland
With the Consumer Association of Ireland
About 300 restaurants assessed by consumers from all over the country. An essential guide for the traveller. *£4.95 paperback.*

THE BLASKET ISLANDS — Next Parish America
Joan and Ray Stagles
The history, characters, social organisation, nature - all aspects of this most fascinating and historical of islands. Illustrated. *£7.95 paperback.*

SKELLIG — Island outpost of Europe
Des Lavelle
Probably Europe's strangest monument from the Early Christian era, this island, several miles out to sea, was the home of an early monastic settlement. Illustrated. *£7.95 paperback.*

DUBLIN — One Thousand Years
Stephen Conlin
A short history of Dublin with unique full colour reconstruction drawings based on the latest research. *Hardback £9.95, paperback £5.95.*